Joanne Kyger

There You Are

Interviews, Journals, and Ephemera

Edited by Cedar Sigo

Wave Books

Seattle and New York

Published by Wave Books
www.wavepoetry.com

Wave Books titles are distributed to the trade by
Consortium Book Sales and Distribution
Phone: 800-283-3572 / SAN 631-760X
Library of Congress Cataloging-in-Publication Data
Names: Kyger, Joanne, author. | Sigo, Cedar, editor.
Title: There you are : interviews, journals, and ephemera / Joanne Kyger ; edited by Cedar Sigo.
Description: First edition. | Seattle : Wave Books, [2017]
Identifiers: LCCN 2017001121 | ISBN 9781940696584 (paperback)
Subjects: LCSH: Kyger, Joanne. | Poets, American—20th century—Biography. | BISAC: LITERARY COLLECTIONS / American / General. | POETRY / American / General.
Classification: LCC PS3561.Y35 Z46 2017 | DDC 811/.54 [B]—dc23
LC record available at https://lccn.loc.gov/2017001121
Cover photo taken in 1968 by Zoe N. Brown
for *Places to Go* (Black Sparrow, 1970).
Designed and composed by Quemadura
Printed in the United States of America
9 8 7 6 5 4 3 2 1
First Edition
Wave Interviews 1

[Joanne Kyger]

Send to Anne VT

There are ways of being in the world that make clear it need not be a place of endless contention or a trial to permit passage to some imagined elsewhere. Poetry, of all the arts, has made insistently articulate all the patterns of human prospect and illusion, but it has also seen, paradoxically, where it is we live literally more than eyes alone have been able to. Because no world, of whatever disposition or proposal, is simply there. It is a human invention and no reality will ever be otherwise.

Early poems of Joanne Kyger's made very clear that her place was not to be the one simply familiar, for that time at least, and her Penelope had no accomodating patience for the vagaries of Odysseus' meandering. In that way she is one of this generation's clarities, that we cannot longer indulge an habituated paternity that wants the authority of force and feels that women are somehow an addenda to the real business of life.

She arrived in excellent and curious company--Jack Spicer and Robert Duncan both recognized her power as elders, and her various brothers, Richard Brautigan and Gary Snyder among them, could understand certainly that she was an unequivocal equal. She brought to poetry a remarkable humor, a wit as deft as one might wish for, and an almost confusing demur in respect to prizes or any such games poets play.

Like Laura Riding, she has had no interest in the usual market place of this art, the anthologies, appointments, etc. Yet this fact has nothing to do with a Puritan austerity of purpose. Rather, she lives so explicitly where she is and with what she has as daily factor, that some projection of it all into the vacant generality of usual ambitions has never been her interest. No doubt it has cost her a general reputation, so to speak, but she of all people would hardly value such an immaterial advantage. She plays a far tighter game, if that's the point.

She lives in an incredible place, some few miles north of San Francisco, on a high bluff just at the sea's edge. She is a Westerner and, as with those friends noted previously, it proves an absolute way of seeing we have known in ways too distracted by the misogony of Robinson Jeffers or the ambition of Kenneth Rexroth, albeit an absolute condition in the work of either. Possibly the force of that specific world is of such order it requires no designation or concern. Her old friend Phillip Whalen put it best in one of his poems: "Let's call it the Pacific." Best one let such wonders speak for themselves.

Robert Creeley
June 6, 1988

Introduction

I.

This book has been blessed with soft, dreamlike edges from the very beginning. I was given a large stack of Joanne Kyger interviews and then asked to cut a continuous shape for them. Though the earliest of the interviews dates from 1974 and the latest to 2014, I have chosen to collage them with an eye on telling Joanne's story chronologically. While I was cutting and fitting the book together I began to feel that I was living out Ezra Pound's proclamation, "In the mind of the poet all times are contemporaneous." I was also haunted by this untitled two-line poem of Joanne's from the early 1970s:

> I'm going to be a poet, I can put it together too.
>
> Life is beset by small accidents.

It becomes obvious when reading through Joanne's work that she has lived and continues to live a very full life. Few artists bestow such a sacred quality of attention upon their surroundings and in the hands of most poets the concept of the "sacred" can become a burden to the poem. Joanne maintains the awareness that imparting such grace requires the lightest touch possible. She can spin her poems with humor and surprise so the sacred is found among the minute particulars of daily life, the bend to the bamboo grove as the wind dies down, greeting visiting poets or greeting the scrub jays and quail that move in and around her property. These details gather together to form an ever-changing ground for her practice, wherein a simple notation can become an act of transmission.

The act of dating her work seems to automatically invite the next poem, as if any utterance in any moment might be worthy of making it down onto the page. Daily writing is often dismissed as indulgent or lacking drama, but what if Joanne is dating her work in order to indicate the stakes involved in continuing to live as a poet, to re-recognize poetry as an element in the world so frequently and then to know that she can't possibly chase it all down in one day? The overflow of light that escapes unused then surrounds her. This becomes the presumed aura of the poet:

> My attention to writing is a daily practice, which then builds an accumulative narrative of chronology. Which ends up as the story of one's life. An historical sense of 'self,' breathing and experiencing what is common to every human—the local, the ordinary, the non-motivated sense of just 'being.' One is also aware of the accumulations of lineage of all those writing persons who have come before and to whom one owes the inheritance of this written moment.

I am always fascinated by the occurrence of the word "form" throughout Joanne's work. I opened her collected poems, *About Now*, at random recently and the first instance I found was in the last stanza of a poem titled "(Out the Window)":

> Tin hearted memories, chemicals.
> We fight through a hideous mishmash of inheritance,
> Forgiving for deeper stamina. That we go on, the world
> always goes on, breaking us with its changes
> until our form, exhausted, runs true.

Here Joanne's reporting back on breaking through becomes the content. How is the poem floated or carried? Her lines are held up primarily through the breath that is issued from our bodies.

In a later poem from 1983, "Day after Ted Berrigan's Memorial Reading," she writes:

> Out back with Dante looking down his nose, kind of low
> limbed anxiety. Sigh. Don splitting cypress
> from huge pile felled last winter.
> Is this the form
>
> I come home to? Yes, and beyond too, oceans
> of paragraphs reiterate the everyday story
> of amazing circumstances in life.

I feel indebted to Joanne for her question, "Is this the form / I come home to?" It delineates exactly what the poet expects of herself (even in grief), and she proceeds to place it right into her poem. When poets speak of "measure" these are the sorts of lines that should be discussed. The poem is not disrupted by including this question but actually gains in transparency. Joanne has often reminded me of a favorite quote from one of her teachers, Chögyam Trungpa Rinpoche, "Writing is writing the mind." This seems to involve hanging onto a landscape as it is being uncovered in language and a willingness to add further contours as they spring to mind. The agency of the poet is such that there is no longer fear of a false note or interruption.

> WHEREVER YOU WALK
> THERE'S A PATH
>
> Returning home find
> feverfew by the door has bloomed

—a welcome committee   from all that
tossed dishwater

Everything in place
naturally 'there'
'as is'
present and perfect

from birth
and after birth
and death and aftermath

When words let go of you
who are you anyway?

Every time you go away

a way opens up

everywhere

you are

where words are your path,

YOUR words   ARE your path.

The poem is dated July 14, 2014. Its form is comprised of Joanne walking around her property after a long trip and taking note of how the landscape has changed. This particular poem opens up to the realization that even away from home she brings the culmination of her practice with her, a personal swath is cut and her line transcends the page so often, it has been permanently propped up to live ahead of her actions. A few weeks after Joanne handed this poem to me I noticed she had used the same form in an earlier piece with entirely different results:

GRATEFUL

After two months in Mexico

and continual rainstorms here
To find this studio

not slurped away by a sub pocket
Of suction hell.   Anyway

notebooks a bit damp
and mold has taken
    the last of the faded blue Atticus

butterfly.   Still *dry* framed
picture of pensive youngster—

'Nobody loves me
I'm going into the garden
to eat worms'

And looking fairly immaculate—

  Trungpa's 'First thought
              Best thought'
    Which makes it seem   easy

   'Yesterday I ate two smooth ones
    And one wooly one.'

February 11, 1998

There is absolutely nothing trapped about Joanne's poetry. In fact, I find its most characteristic quality is the turning of perception made manifest in her voice. When a poet stays attuned to the possibilities of the present moment any attempt at summing up is impossible. The intention is to keep her voice active. The overtones that drift up and off of her phrasing are exquisite. They hold her audience so closely and at the same time require a clear physical carving into space. A break in the line may indicate a pause in the rhythm while the layout on the page tells us how long that pause should last. This is the ever elusive quality of *suspension* at work. I can think of no other poet who has so inhabited Charles Olson's claim, "Art does not seek to describe but to enact."

II.

Making up a literary history is the phenomena of looking back and trying to make a picture of a puzzle.

Born in Vallejo, California, in 1934, Joanne Kyger had a typically nomadic Navy childhood. The family sailed for China when she was six weeks old and returned when she was almost three to Pensacola, Florida and then to Long Beach, California, Lake Bluff, Illinois, Upper Darby, Pennsylvania. Finally, at the age of fourteen her family returned to California, settling in Santa Barbara for the next eight years. She enrolled at the University of California at Santa Barbara where she studied philosophy and literature before moving to San Francisco in 1957.

From 1957–1969 Joanne continued to be quite restless and covered a lot of ground. Just three years after she came to San Francisco she moved to Kyoto to live with Gary Snyder then traveled through India and back to Japan. She sailed home to San Francisco in 1964 and stayed for a year. During this time she took part in the 1965 Berkeley Poetry Conference. She then went to Europe for eight months with Jack Boyce in February 1966 and then lived in New York City for nine months. After returning to San Francisco in September 1967 she spent ten months working on experimental television at KPFA. After the summer of 1968, she spent time in Lagunitas and Bodega Bay before moving to land in Bolinas in the spring of 1969. Although there were a few writers like Bill Brown, Tom Clark, and John Thorpe already living in Bolinas, it was after Joanne's arrival that other poets and artists began to arrive en masse, some to live and others to visit. The esteemed list includes Robert Creeley, Jim Carroll, Bill Berkson, Lewis and Phoebe MacAdams, Richard Brautigan, Ebbe Borregaard, David Meltzer, Bobbie Louise Hawkins, Duncan McNaughton, Philip Whalen, Arthur Okamura, Joe Brainard, and Ken Botto. This history has largely been told in fits and starts:

> *Then again writers, poets whose lives have been close to you are often who your dialog is with. They may not necessarily be in your vicinity anymore but they are where your thoughts go, your family as it were. From this comes an intimacy of tone which includes the reader.*

I have been taking great pleasure in forming a select list of books that include Joanne as a presence. In the end the list partially consists of:

707 Scott Street by John Wieners
Passage through India by Gary Snyder
Happiness Bastard by Kirby Doyle
You Didn't Even Try and *Imaginary Speeches for a Brazen Head* (novels) by Philip Whalen
Robert Duncan in San Francisco by Michael Rumaker
Bolinas Journal by Joe Brainard

When it came time to put the portraits, letters, and poetry into this book Joanne placed the interviews around her dining room table so that we could see exactly what we were making. It was only after we settled on how to bring her friends along that the book began to feel complete.

Friends I've loved
all the time,
Joanne,
Shao—but

not so
simply
now
to name them

(Robert Creeley, from *Hello*)

III.

It has been twenty years since Joanne and I were staying in the same odd sorority house in Boulder, Colorado. It was the summer of 1996 and I was a scholarship student at the Naropa Institute. One night I found her bounding up and down the halls opening every drawer and closet door. When I asked her what she was doing she simply said she was "looking for something . . . *useful*!"

We exchanged a few letters after I returned to Suquamish. I had decided to take a job at our tribal museum in order to save up money to study at Naropa year round. In her first letter Joanne suggested that I read the work of John Wieners, writing that "in the last few years, of course, he has gone completely mad." I dutifully took the ferry boat over to Seattle and purchased Wieners' *Selected Poems*. When I moved out to San Francisco in 1999 at the age of twenty-one I managed to find a small room at the Stanley Hotel near the corner of Polk and California Street. The rent was 550 dollars a month. Once I got the phone connected I immediately called Joanne and told her what my cross streets were. She said, "Oh, you're right by the Hotel Wentley." This single fact held me fascinated and soon I was seeking out other landmarks of San Francisco poetry history. I also began to reread John's *Selected Poems* and they came to life all over again with a sharp clarity.

I walk under the distant stars
as I did when a child with my brother; as I did
with Wallace on Grant Street in those long, cool

San Francisco nights, that seemed
to have no edges—
only avenues
of columns and evergreens
without walls

(John Wieners, from *Ace of Pentacles*)

I would get out to Joanne's house as often as I could find a ride up to Bolinas and back. During my first handful of visits Joanne always made sure that Dave Haselwood was in attendance. Dave and I got along famously, and soon I began to collect the books he published on Auerhahn Press in the late fifties and early sixties: *The Hotel Wentley Poems* by John Wieners, Philip Whalen's *Memoirs of an Interglacial Age*, Michael McClure's *Dark Brown*, Diane di Prima's *The New Handbook of Heaven*, Jack Spicer's *The Heads of the Town up to the Aether*, Philip Lamantia's *Ekstasis* and *Destroyed Works*. Talking with Dave about the artists he used for the covers of his books helped to extend my sense of poetic history into the realm of the visual arts. The work of Wallace Berman led to that of Bruce Conner which led to Jess then Kenneth Anger. Each Auerhahn volume was such a considered object that the books moved beyond the realm of design, they felt destined.

Just before Christmas 1999 Joanne sent a copy of *The Dharma Committee* to my hotel. Every weekday the building manager would push the mail under the door to my room. The book is 8½ × 11 inches, stapled up the side with a light purple cover and pink lead in pages, a stated third printing by Smithereens Press. The cover is a drawing by Joanne's husband, Donald Guravich, based on a W. W. Denslow drawing of the Oz characters. The book reads like a mock exposé on the Spicer circle, and it helped me to further visualize their comings and goings.

> A new Dharma Committee rule reads as follows;
> "DHARMA COMMITTEE MEMBERS DO NOT HAVE TO SLEEP, EVER."
>
> George Stanley, Russ Fitzgerald, Jack Moore, Joanne Kyger have found a new way to look at stars. It is flat on your back drunk on Mt. Tamalpais with a rip in the seat of your leotards at 3:30 AM with Kirby Doyle raging down the streets of Sausalito because he cannot think of hideous enough death for afore mentioned members of the Dharma Committee.
>
> George Stanley exists only at the whim of the Dharma Committee and Jack Spicer.

Joanne also attended the fabled Sunday meetings at which young poets would read their work aloud to both Spicer and Robert Duncan. They would meet in various apartments around the city but the poets present stayed the same. It was with this group in February 1958 that Joanne unveiled her first instant classic, "The Maze," with its quick-shifting and short line one can feel a sense of enclosure, of vibrant daylight and the sky overhead. It seems to live in my memory more as a film than a poem. Duncan wrote a fourteen page letter to George Stanley concerning both "The Maze" as well as "The Door Poem" by Harold Dull. The letter expanded to become a rolling defense of Duncan's own poetics and was published by White Rabbit Press in 1964 under the title *As Testimony: The Poem & the Scene*:

> As in the scene Sunday I see Joanne Kyger kneeling. There had been a chair, but she sits always on the floor, not crouching Sunday, on her knees as the poem was read.
>
> . . . Where we refer to antiquity names have power too. In the Maze poem Joanne had read—"*I saw the bird / on the sidewalk / his neck naked / as in prehistory*" this is how I read it, reciting it to Hal and Dory today. But Hal corrected me: *prehistoric* it had said. Slowly, to discover the design we must find the exact word, the exact name . . .
>
> . . . Joanne Kyger's poem began "I saw"; the sound of awe lingerd as a base tone (where the word *awe* never emerges) thru the diminished ô of walk, all, fall, water (for the sound of water was that sound rushing) on to the close with the word *walls*. "And so I walkd" she writes, "wanting to fall."

Joanne was first published in issue 4 of Jack Spicer's *J* magazine in October 1959. Spicer collected poems for the magazine from a box marked "J" in The Place, a favorite bar on Grant Avenue in North Beach. It was a short poem eventually included in her first book, *The Tapestry and the Web*. The periods at both ends of the line are meant to indicate a breath stop.

TAPESTRY

the eye

is drawn

to the bold

DESIGN —— the

.Border.

.California flowers.

nothing promised that isn't shown.

Implements:

shell

stone

.Peacock.

On March 6, 2015, I attended Joanne's reading at the San Francisco Poetry Center to celebrate her latest book, *On Time*. That night the titles of her poems were whispered, or spoken from afar. It was as if the interruption of the titles might break down the hushed, intimate tones that her voice was intent on forming. This gesture felt disarming in its simplicity, an opening out from the center with a sudden pause built in. I began to realize over the course of this reading that the discipline of the practice itself secures her architecture. Joanne's poetry is not so dependent on good or bad lines but upon the vantage point that she starts from:

WINDOW LEDGE

Tiny light grey moth
        New Delhi bronze rabbit
                Roy de Forest dog
                        Kwan Yin
      Lady of white,
pottery shards from Palomarin shell mound
Miwok obsidian scraper, gourd pebble
from Boulder Creek, silver and white
streaked rock from Santa Barbara
Light grey moth

Cedar Sigo
August 15, 2016

There You Are

Interview with Paul Watsky, *Jung Journal*

Paul Watsky: I'd like to explore the question of how you became you, the woman of what has been termed, "A disciplined openness," who by her early twenties, despite being raised in the household of a career naval officer, was one of a very few females accepted by the San Francisco coterie of radically unconventional male poets, many of whom were unabashedly gay.

You, yourself, have said that during the 1950s, "Very few women set out to be independent thinkers," and that in those days you "didn't find many women I could talk to in any interesting way, who thought about being intellectually independent—or making that a goal or aim."

What were you like as a little kid?

Joanne Kyger: I learned to read when we moved to Lake Bluff, Illinois, in 1941. I was five years old. And from then on everything was an "awakening." I learned to read. I learned to write, play the violin, ride a bicycle, ice skate, experience the seasons, see "nature." We stayed through my sixth grade. I found everything I needed to know. Lake Bluff was a really small town with a library. I think that's why I like Bolinas, because it has a small town's circumference, it's intimate, and has a great library.

Learning to read was wonderful. I was an insane reader. I read everything I could. I would take out thirteen books at a time, all that the basket on my bicycle would hold. I read really fast. I would read up and down the page, skip a lot of words in between if I didn't understand them. Thank God there wasn't any television then. I probably would have been glued to it.

My closest relations were my mother and two sisters. My father was in the war during the early Forties. In 1949, we moved to Santa Barbara, where I went to high school. I had some excellent teachers, one on the school newspaper where I was the features editor, and Henry Brubeck, the orchestra leader, who was Dave Brubeck's brother. I played second violin valiantly. Then I went on to UC Santa Barbara, where I had some more excellent teachers: Hugh Kenner, who taught Ezra Pound and William Carlos Williams, and Paul Wienpahl, who taught Wittgenstein and Heidegger. He showed us how Heidegger's "nothing" was the bridge into D. T. Suzuki's Buddhist nothingness.

My early home life: a bit chaotic. My parents stayed together for twelve years of marriage, and my father was away in the war about three years of that time. Mostly, it was my mother and my two sisters that comprised the household.

What kind of people were your parents?

Well, my mother was a Canadian, from a family of eleven, who had moved down to Long Beach around 1914. There had been a big economic downturn in the part of Canada they were from. My grandfather had been a grocery store owner. They were Irish and Scotch—Callin and Lamont. There was a big migration of Canadians down to Long Beach. At one point it had the largest population of Canadians outside Canada.

What part of Canada was your mother's family from?

Saskatchewan. Saskatoon, Saskatchewan.

So they were sort of plains people, in a sense. What kind of personality did she have?

She was the youngest daughter and had a younger brother. She was pretty, but vain, my aunts told me.

Did she express much affection?

Yes, but it was irregular. I do think that she wanted everybody to succeed and feel well. We all ended up in a little house in Santa Barbara in 1949. It was a female-driven household. My mother went back to work for the first time in fifteen years.

Your parents split up permanently or temporarily?

The legal separation was permanent. He went down to San Diego where many retired naval officers ended up.

Do you remember what that was like for you when that happened?

Relief, because then we didn't hear the quarreling anymore. My father was the youngest of thirteen and was twelve years older than my mother. He was already a heavy drinker by the time they met. He essentially wasn't a family man.

Did he pay any attention to you?

Yes, he had a kind of an old-fashioned gracefulness of language. He was from Virginia. His father, my grandfather, who I never met, fought in the Civil War when he was eighteen, and then went on to be both major and sheriff of Elkton, Virginia. My father had these great Southern manners. He loved to play golf, but I don't think he felt very comfortable at home. I remember my mother saying frequently that he "wasn't very good around the house." The last household we had together was in Upper Darby, Pennsylvania, before he resigned from the Navy. We had dinners, these endless dinners, during which we would be practically interrogated in what passed as dinner table conversation. "What did you do today at school? What did you learn?" etc. I think he was always slightly loaded, and the Officers' Club seemed to be more interesting for him. So we ended up in Santa Barbara when I was about twelve. After I went to college I finally was able to get my own place, when I was about twenty. Everything at home seemed to be emotionally fraught, very emotionally volatile.

How did that affect you as a kid growing up?

When you're little you take refuge, and you take refuge in books, in your room. I was the older sister so I got my own room. You make friends and visit them.

Did you have any particularly memorable friends?

I did. I had friends I loved in Upper Darby and friends in Lake Bluff. I had to start over again in Santa Barbara, making friends, finding my way around. It was a big cultural jump. I wrote for the school newspaper, I was in the orchestra, so I had these other social contacts.

Were you a naturally outgoing kid?

I think there were two responses: I could be naturally outgoing, and then there was the retreat, back into the corner in which you try to find some refuge and privacy.

When would you do that, under what circumstances?

At the end of a long day, what's better than getting to your room and reading a book and just kind of—

In Jung's terminology, that makes it likely you were an introvert—

With extroverted qualities. I always wrote for the school newspaper, writing features and humorous columns and things like that through high school and into college, so that was always a way of giving a particular voice. It was more of an extroverted kind of presentation. I was willing to put my name to it.

Would you go out and do a lot of interviewing and gathering facts relating to your subjects?

Yes, often. And then I just wrote my own column, so a lot of my imagination was at play in what was going on.

Certainly your poetry suggests that you do a fair amount of both, the introverted and the extroverted side of things.

Bolinas was an example of needing to be part of a community—and in order for this larger social body to function well you let your "ego" drop aside, which taught me a lot in the forty years I've been here. So it's a little bit of both.

When you began discovering yourself as a sexual being, what was that like?

Well, there were grade school and high school crushes, which were very funny. I realized having a crush or a fixation on somebody was really delightful. Just reading through some yearbook inscriptions recently, I see a wide variety of recipients. My first boyfriends were very sweet. Then I had a longer relationship when I was in college, and when that ended it was like a heartbreak for me. It was my first sense of emotional devastation and how to deal with it psychologically. How did you heal yourself? I don't know if, in some way, anyone ever does from one's first real heartbreak.

Then, of course, there were interesting relationships in San Francisco, which were minimal, until I set out for Japan. I was twenty-six years old when I left California in February of 1960. I went to Kyoto and lived there for over four years because I was really interested in studying Buddhism. At that point, that was my direction. "Psychology" wasn't working for me. (I was going to group therapy, where the psychologist thought sitting meditation was anal retentive.) But I found meditation to be a very calming activity, and by this point Japanese meditation seemed a very centered solution. Since I had spent the first three years of my life in China, the Orient didn't seem like a totally big step. I was stepping off the West Coast again and to a direction that would give me some clarity.

Mixed into that I'd taken a few peyote trips, one in Marin and one over La Rocca's Bar in San Francisco, where I was renting an apartment. It was there that I had a really colossal schizophrenic, devastating trip in which I went in and out of these states of reality. I was with two other people. I fell into "nothingness," lightning flashes, then people had animal faces. I mean, really. Please. I'm over La Rocca's Mafia Bar.

Scary.

It was scary. It was scary. And I kept having flashbacks for the next year. It was a very schizophrenic episode, and essentially I spent the next four years getting through what that was all about.

You were twenty-five or twenty-six when that happened?

It was February of 1959. I was twenty-five. I was never quite sure just how strong "my" consciousness was. So in Japan there was always this little teetering of, "Oh, oh, am I going to fall into the void again?" until I finally understood that some of these scary places were just like guardian figures. They were states of mind.

How did that become clear to you?

Well, I was looking at these Kamakura Warrior guardian figures outside temples there, and realized they were only frightening if you were afraid to go beyond them. To enter into the temple. They were protectors—not figures to get hung up on. I related this understanding to Carlos Castaneda after I returned, who was visiting with Michael Harner over at my editor Don Allen's house.

You just met everybody.

Well, not everybody. I didn't meet Mick Jagger. I realized that Castaneda was familiar with the same kind of demonic energies, the power of them. By that point, I think I had really understood that these were states of mind that were just holding you back, that they were not there forever. They were illusion. Let's put it that way.

That was after you came back from Japan?

After I returned I stopped being so nervous about the "self" and where one's mind could take you, whether you were going to go crazy, and what is "crazy" in essence. During my early San Francisco years, I was also taking Dexedrine—prescribed for me by a psychiatrist when I was in college—"mother's little helpers," to get through daytime working and nighttime celebrations.

You weren't getting enough sleep?

No! Getting very spun out.

If I could back you up a couple of notches. You majored in philosophy? What attracted you to that?

I was part of an experimental program called the "tutorial program," which meant that we had certain teachers who were willing to meet individually with students on a study course of their own choosing—

writing papers and reading their own curriculum. University of California at Santa Barbara had just moved the campus from the Riviera in Santa Barbara up to Goleta on the coast. I did that for the last two years in school. But I still had to take freshman biology, with its lab course, and I just couldn't memorize all the phylums and things like that, and so I flunked it and was short one unit for graduation. I just said, "Oh, well, phooey. I already have rented a place in San Francisco. I'm just going to move up there. I'll go back later and take that lab course," but I never did.

So you hadn't had a fundamental desire to be a philosopher?

Not if it involved a degree. My philosophy teacher, Paul Wienpahl, was of great interest to me. He was trying to take this Logical Positivism of dry contemporary Western philosophy to a next step—into Buddhist thinking and practice. D. T. Suzuki talks about "nothing" or "emptiness" as really being "something." As Philip Whalen says, "Emptiness is Full of Everything."

There was a whole body of wisdom out there, at the time called Western philosophy, that was doing no one any "good." I mean, they were reduced to discussing in these little philosophy journals such topics as, "You have a headache and you've taken aspirin and the headache goes away. Is the headache still really there or only being 'hidden' by the aspirin?" I thought, "I want to know about life. I need to know what my being is about. I need to know more than this." It was all ending up with language talking about language.

Would there be one or two principles that particularly spoke to you in what Suzuki was saying that made you feel like the Eastern mind could provide you with something that you weren't getting back in the US?

Oh, well, I hadn't quite left yet. I don't think I referred to "the Eastern mind" then. There was a kind of schizophrenic dualism, a Cartesian mind/body dualism that needed to be resolved for me. There was also the religious aspect of Christianity—sin and suffering—versus some more serene sense of Buddhism, although I didn't quite know what Buddhism really was then. I thought I knew what Zen Buddhism was about. Zen Buddhists pointed out that concepts, ideas, are just ephemeral, so what really exists is you in the moment. And all those Buddhist writings and sutras written down on pieces of paper were really nothing but toilet paper (Rinzai Gigen).

That was very appealing, of course, to a California mind, along with what D. T. Suzuki, Alan Watts, and others were writing about. There was a real possibility of freedom of the moment. Of course, after going to Japan, I realized you had to learn how to make a place in which you could have that freedom, that freedom had walls. In other words, you had to understand what a structure was, which meant that, yes, you got up early in the morning and you sat meditation, and that you tried to focus your mind, to empty it. You observed your mind enough to know that it was ceaselessly busy. It wasn't going to go anywhere, and it could do anything it wanted. But if you kept going back and centering yourself, then you could see that this mind, which could be a demon towards you or whip you around, was of the moment, something that you could accept and let it pass on.

Well, accept certain things as your experience and valid as such, but not necessarily the final word on anything.

Right. You see those "states of mind" as just another illusion. Allen Ginsberg asked the Tibetan teacher Dudjom Rinpoche about what to do with some dreadful visions he was having and got some really practical advice: "If you see anything horrible, don't cling to it; if you see anything beautiful, don't cling to it." Just let it go by. No place to hold onto.

That Japan trip, did your expectations come to pass? Did it turn out to be what you wanted?

I don't know what I wanted, exactly. I set out to have a relationship within Japan, and with Japan. Gary Snyder told me at one point that he really felt that he needed a Western mind, a woman's mind, to be with him, an intellectual companion. After four years, we went back to the United States, and I was so relieved to get out of that particular very strict environment that I realized that I probably wasn't going to go back. But sure enough, after he returned again to Japan for the third time, Gary did find a very attractive young Japanese lady to marry and have two children with. I could tell that he really loved Japanese culture and was at home with it in a way that I was not.

You were in Japan but you did not become of *Japan in a certain sense.*

I loved all the folk art of Japan. I fell in love with the Japanese folk craft pottery that came from the Mingei movement. A lot of foreigners over there on Fulbrights studying that tradition became friends of mine. Gary's monkish tradition dictated, "No more than two teacups," or something like that. "What if I want five?" But he was living a very disciplined kind of life, and I was thinking more in terms of a household, which I still do. We had these two rooms, a bath, and a teeny kitchen in a lovely little house. He always prepared for sanzen at four in the morning. I still didn't have a teacher in that more formal practice of Rinzai Zen. My Japanese was nowhere near adequate. Yes, I think living there was in many ways very restrictive for me. When we came back in 1964, I realized that there was all this California freedom to do what I wanted, and everyone spoke English! It was just too heady. Don Allen told me he wanted to publish my first book of poems. It was great. I just couldn't believe I was here.

It does seem, from your journal, you struggled a fair amount in Japan with loneliness and anxiety. And my impression was that it opened up some old wounds related to your mother because you describe her in the journal as having "never breast fed me—she didn't have enough."

Well, this was my attempt at doing some kind of psychological analysis. I don't think I ever got along with my mother very well. She was the kind of person who could turn around really quick. She was Irish in that way. I recently wrote, "I don't like her very much, but I don't want to be left behind." What are you going to do? Some people have really nice people as mothers. I think I was just trying to get disentangled. What was the sense of trying to blame my mother for things? Perhaps it's my over analysis saying, "Oh, well, I didn't get breast fed," or analyzing some anxious sensation of being thirsty. I was whisked off to China when I was six weeks old, with a baby bottle.

There's your 1962 entry, "Perhaps I killed my mother. She lay dead on the bed like Nastasya Filippovna at the end of The Idiot, *which I finished yesterday." Well, Nastasya was quite a piece of work, a tormented woman—and tormenting. She apparently was based on a mistress of Dostoyevsky's who never read his books. But the way you're describing your mother so far doesn't sound like she had that malignant intensity.*

She could go off on tirades, temper tantrums. The dream figure of the crazy woman in the attic could be her, but I realized I could be the crazy woman in my own attic. Anyway there was somebody up there running amok. I learned, because of her emotional makeup, never to trust her in a certain way, because you could never tell when something was going to be turned around and be thrown back at you, just twisted somehow. And she enjoyed arguments and fighting. She just wanted to stir it up. It was uncomfortable emotionally.

It sounds like you may have figured out some ways to raise yourself and grow yourself up. It's my impression neither of your parents was giving you too much help.

It was pathetic. I was still always trying to calm her down, say things that would be pleasing to her, blah, blah, blah, even to just living here, where I do now. Where she never visited me. So I did, obviously, want some emotional support from her. How do you cut yourself off? You can't really, especially if someone really wants you to be there, especially as she wrote letters at least weekly.

This, I think, testifies to a kind of generosity of spirit. For you it would not be conceivable to cut your mother off, no matter how annoying she was, and that does you credit.

That's nice of you. "I don't want to be left behind."

That gives it a negative cast, but from what you say I think it's hard for you to leave other people behind. In March '63, after three years in Japan, you write, "There's nothing here that I have ever been attracted to, and Gary is no one I can depend on completely."

I don't know if I really meant it. I think I was just writing it out to see what it sounded like.

Any reappraisals?

I remember after a party we had in Kyoto, there was this very cute girl there that he was flirting with. I mean, many people came to see him. But I was especially bothered by girls with long blonde hair. I think it's the first time I saw what groupies would be like.

So this was a statement of the moment.

A little overstated. Of course, there were many things and people I was attracted to in Japan. It was a depressed entry. I think I wanted to feel more included. But I also wanted to be independent. Intellectually independent. Emotionally probably not so successful, but I think I certainly felt intellectually independent. I had my own ideas about things, and Philip Whalen was a constant correspondent and support, so I felt that I wasn't out on a limb by myself. I never depended on Snyder for, "Is this good or bad writing?" During this time, I was developing my own "voice." Looking for my own "way," a direction I could feel comfortable with.

It's my impression from reading the diary that he wasn't a kind of meet-you-halfway, split-the-difference kind of guy, that he had very much his view of how things had to be.

I think, for his own direction, yes. He was very disciplined in his Zen practice. He had a teacher, and this was a demanding relationship. He was also a mature poet by that point. He had published *Myths and Texts*, and then *Rip Rap*, which were his amalgam of Buddhist/Native American work-ethic poems that were very particular to the Pacific Rim. They were unique.

He was also very private. Ginsberg wanted to be part of a larger, revolutionary Beat movement. He always knew how to talk to the media. He made a public persona of himself, whereas Snyder was private. He was studying this Buddhist path in which he was very strict with himself. But he was also a wonderfully humorous, jovial, amusing friend to be with.

Ah, I didn't get so much of a sense of that from the diary.

It's unfortunate, you know, how often one writes in a journal to complain.

Do you have any recollections of him kidding around?

There are some pictures in the journal, which I put in to show a lighter side. There's one of a kind of indoor leg stretching yoga party. And one in which Snyder is using the slide projector as an infernal ray gun.

In Japan, you wrote, "The fact that things change has always been a source of worry and depression to me." In April 1960, you ask, "Is this my home? Have I ever had a home?" Did your migration in 1969, to Bolinas, with your second husband, Jack Boyce, to a small community in Western Marin County north of San Francisco, did that resolve the issue?

In some way it did. I had this professor from Santa Barbara who came over, to Japan, and I remember him saying, "Things always change." And I thought, "Good Lord. No!" He was an economics teacher. Somehow I thought I was entering into stability. The Buddhist teaching of impermanence and change hadn't sunk home. Really.

So he brought you bad news.

I think moving around a lot when I was young was destabilizing. Back in 1969, Bolinas was very open in terms of what the counterculture was about. People were doing all sorts of wonderful things—and sometimes doing things that just didn't turn out so well.

Jack Boyce and Lew Welch, both having left San Francisco, met up in the Forks of Salmon in Siskiyou County in the early '60s and became friends. Then they moved back to San Francisco in 1964, where I met Jack after I had returned from Japan. Lew Welch died or "disappeared" up by Snyder's land in '71, and the next year, 1972, Jack died here in Bolinas.

They were partners in doing what?

Probably in telling each other their life history and how to cure civilization. Lew would come over, and they would drink a bottle of whisky, and Lew would read Gertrude Stein to him. They would do back-woodsman things with knives and axes and fishing rods. Jack would do his paintings, and Lew wrote poems. Then Lew would bring him on visits to San Francisco to meet his poet friends. That's how I was introduced to Jack. I knew he had had a head injury while playing high school football, coupled with a crazy kind of erratic sense of justice. Anyway, Lew disappeared in '71 with his gun, and the next year Jack was gone, too, walked along the roof beam of his house that he was building, but didn't make it to the end. That was a scary time.

He fell and was killed?

Yes.

And Lew Welch walked into the woods and nobody ever found him?

He was trying to build a house up there at Gary's, and he just couldn't do it. He was really what we now call bipolar, a severely alcoholic person at that point. He even took Antabuse and was drinking.

Would you and Jack have called it quits between the two of you at some point?

It was like everybody that came to Bolinas during that time lasted about a year and then they separated. I don't know if you remember back to those times, but there was a lot of leaving or changing of partners in the communities. After a year I moved out. We had been together about six years.

I don't remember Bolinas specifically. I was teaching at San Francisco State. I came back out to California in '69, and yes, there was a lot of community expectation that relationships weren't for the long haul, that they weren't going to last. The big destabilizer of the people I knew at State was feminism. The women were forming communities with each other frequently, women who were in relationships with men but who became very, very critical of the relationships, and the guys, and what was happening between them.

Really. Of course, out here you had to band together in different ways, because it was just these tiny mesa houses with teeny septic tanks, and rutty dirt roads. There were a lot of welfare mothers, single mothers with children, and a lot of trying to build community and keep a free and active school. Taking care of your daily existence often was what you did every day, all you had time for. But there were other activities too.

I remember the women's peyote meetings. All these women came and took peyote, in this big open-air house. It was kind of a funny experience. I don't think anybody knew what "ceremony" to follow. Someone asked, "What should I do? There's all these women." And someone else answered, "Well, just pretend half of them are men."

How often did those take place?

I think there were one or two. There were also meetings out at RCA Beach.

So this was the actual eating of the peyote buttons and the throwing up from the strychnine and stuff like that? Was there any religious component? Native religion going on?

Everyone was very respectful, and I think various protocols and songs and rituals shaped themselves over time. Peyote has its own truth. It's hard to misuse it.

Well, you had that catastrophic trip that you described over the mob bar. How did you decide to take a shot again after that?

Let me see. Alan Watts brought some mescaline when he came to Kyoto. By that point I was in a healthier place. Everybody took a little bit of the mescaline. I remember him saying to his companion, "Just go with it. Just go with it." I think she was looking at an insect eating a leaf, and the whole universe seemed to be devourable. At that point I realized I wasn't going to tip over into this hell place anymore, so I thought, "Okay, I think my groundwork is a little stronger." After that I came back to the United States, where LSD was around, and mescaline, and mushrooms—all aids for trips and travels, investigations of the spirit.

I could handle what I saw and was able to experience this wonderful expanded sense of self in the world. I mean, you become aware of the interconnectedness of everything. It could be a very wonderful, magical, intuitive experience.

So despite all the disruptions, Bolinas has really felt like a safe home for you and a community where you could be supported and sustained?

Yes.

You've been mentioning as we talk, and also a bit in your writings, that there was a lot of drug use?

We called them psychotropic or psychedelic substances, not just "drugs"—to distinguish them from "harder" substances such as the methamphetamine disasters that were also happening. Ginsberg spoke of the "duty" of the poet to expand consciousness.

My father was a drinker, but it was never served in our household, and my mother didn't drink then. But I was always around people, poets, who were drinking after I went to school and then moved to

San Francisco. Lots of California red and white wine, ninety-nine cents a gallon. But there were disasters like Jack Spicer, Lew Welch, and Jack Kerouac.

Drinking can be a charming sociable practice, or it can be demonic. I'm always paying attention to where it can take you. In lieu of giving it up altogether, I still find a good wine makes situations warm and sweetly domestic, and try to avoid the situations where it turns one into a mad raver. There were several years in Bolinas when it was a long social party. I thought that's what we were supposed to do every day.

I think I was used to living in the atmosphere of North Beach, where people often drank until they reached heights of delirium by performing more and more outrageous acts, and that was delightful. It was different in Japan, where people if they drank too much sake went berserk.

You mean they went berserk in a different way?

They did. They fell apart. Their faces got red and they wept and had to be taken home.

You've now been together for a long time with Donald Guravich, and I don't really know how the two of you met.

We met in Naropa in 1977. I was there teaching. His father had died a few years earlier. He had gone down and spent time in Mexico, traveling. And then he decided to study writing at this new Tibetan Buddhist school in Boulder. Vajrayana Buddhism, with Chögyam Trungpa, carried a lot of energy and charisma. When Allen Ginsberg joined him in 1974, to make a writing program—The Jack Kerouac School of Disembodied Poetics—it seemed like a very attractive direction of study. Anyway, Donald came to Naropa in '77. We hit it off, and he came out here in the spring of '78.

So he came to Bolinas specifically to be with you?

Right. His parents and family were from New Brunswick. Canadians. He's a very warm, intelligent, gracious person.

And wanting to relate. That's the thing that you were looking for.

Before, I had lived here for six years with Peter Warshall, whom I had gone to Desecheo with. He became involved with the community's water and septic issues, wrote for *The Whole Earth Catalogue* and *Whole Earth Review*.

Was he also a warm person?

Yes, very charismatic, very charming.

It certainly seems like the men you've connected with have had certain powers, either as artists or as scientists. They've had a lot going on in their psyches—

Exactly.

Jack Boyce, who we were talking about earlier, he was a painter.

Yes, and a carpenter too.

These have been dynamic guys.

I think so, yes.

That, perhaps, says something about your animus energy, too.

My animus?

To be out there making something happen . . . Let's finish up, if you don't mind, just talking a bit about your poetry. In a poem that's called, "The storms of the season make me loose my reason."

"Lose." I spelled it wrong.

I know. The beginning is all about that. I didn't quite know how I was supposed to write the word, as spelled or intended. That's a 1997 poem, and in there you say of yourself, "I want to be relevant and interior also." Does this still apply?

Of course.

Yes, I didn't think that would change. Relevant and interior—that's the combination we were talking about concerning the introvert and the extrovert. They're both happening. Andrew Schelling, it may have been, who described you as a poet of the moment, and your collected poems are entitled About Now. *At times you've talked as if Trungpa's pronouncement, "first thought best thought," something that Ginsberg picked up on and promulgated widely, was your mantra as well, but you also have written, "I refuse to rewrite this, but I did." How would you describe your long-term relationship with the conflicting ideals of spontaneity and craftswomanship?*

I always remember when Allen said, "If mind is shapely, art is shapely."

That's good stuff.

You accept what comes forth. You accept it. You're not trying to edit yourself. There are certain minimal standards of rewriting, like if I misspell something, which is frequently. I do a little tightening here and there, but I don't think you can really rewrite certain sentences or phrases. You lose the flow. You lose the spontaneity and syllables and inflections and vowels.

Okay, but what I'm hearing you say, and it's really remarkable to me, given just how polished your poetry seems, that it's not built up out of multiple drafts. That's a great ability you've got. I couldn't write that way.

Well, you could.

Yes, but it wouldn't be anything I'd want to read, or anybody else, because I have to do a lot of figuring out and restructuring and pushing things around.

You must have that down by now.

What I've got down by now is more of a resignation to circumstance. If I put something away in a drawer for several weeks before looking at it again, I'll often react, "Oh, my God. Did I write that?" Then I'll see ways to fix it, bring it up a bit. Experience has schooled me to be, I feel, very, very shaky going with drafts where I'd only corrected the spelling or some such. That's just me. Ben Jonson said of Shakespeare that he hardly blotted a line.

Well, he confidently "flowed" right along.

Early on, from friend poets like John Wieners, I learned if you make a mistake, what you call a "mistake," just change the poem so it incorporates it. If you start to misspell a word, find a word that fits that misspelling. It's a practice I've had for a long time, that whatever you write down is "religious" in a certain way, that the word wants to be there. So if you've got that respect for what your utterances are about, you don't try to change it very much. At least it's what John practiced, and I respect that. I think you can learn by restructuring and rewriting, but you lose some "tenderness." Like pastry handled too much becomes tougher. If you have a lot of flaky lines, airy lines so that some wind can blow through them, it's a nice experience. Do you write it by hand?

Yes, I do the first drafts, and then I put them in a computer and move the draft around.

Once you've got a computer, let me tell you, there's a lot of difference in being able to make changes, make corrections, without having to retype a whole page. I was too lazy to retype long poems and tried to use "white-out" judiciously. Sometimes it's just small movements of the line one wants changed very slightly, just to get it so it flows right. But with a computer, whew!—slam bam, you can move lines all over the place.

Do you think that's a corrupting force or a luxury?

I think you get used to putting your voice down a certain way, the phrasing, the way you want a line to move. I always try to write my line so it reflects some movement of inflection.

It seems to me that there's tremendous grace and balance in your work, and all with a single draft—extraordinary.

That new little book I just gave you, *2012*, is partly a composite from notebooks from last year. Certain singular lines felt authentic to me and I chose to let them follow each other on the page. But there are big jumps between subjects, which don't necessarily follow logically in terms of a coherent narrative. It reads like a series of headlines. You can tell me what you think.

I look forward to reading it.

More like a little bulletin board of messages.

I wanted to ask you if there's a meaningful distinction in your mind between the poetry you write and what would be called "academic poetry"?

Since many of my friends who were writing what was called "experimental" poetry are now teachers and "of the academy," what is the academy anymore? In the '50s and '60s, if you were living on the West Coast, you were probably writing in the style of one of the many strands that comprised the San Francisco Renaissance. This was not what was being written and published in the East Coast academic journals, in the *Hudson Review* or *Partisan Review*, or—

But back then that seems to have been an important distinction to your poet friends. I was thinking it was just around the end of the '60s that, say, out of Boston you've got Sylvia Plath and Anne Sexton who were close to Robert Lowell, who himself was bipolar. In your way of thinking would they be academic poets?

I don't think so, but it seems the "academy" at this point has claimed them. Who's not in the academy. You know?

Yes. Well, you're not.

Really? I did teach often at the New College of San Francisco, and have taught at Naropa since 1975, at their Summer Writing Program. But often there are critical "academic" requirements—writing papers, analyzing poetry, and taking poems apart in certain ways, to comment on them—that just seemed to me a ruthless and useless activity.

In the middle 1950s you began to get creative writing departments as well as literature departments. And the people who write the papers about poetry and take it apart are in the literature departments, while the creative writing people, they're supposed to write their poetry and then workshop it, but they don't critique it in the same way.

I know. I just looked at an article in *Poets & Writers*, "Can You Teach Creative Writing?" It's a hard one. "Workshopping" is another useless activity as far as I'm concerned.

Even as we are doing this interview, a conference called AWP is taking place in Boston.

In Boston, right.

I just saw an e-mail from somebody I know who's there. He said there are 12,000 people.

It's a big deal. I mean, I have friends that must go there to get jobs teaching.

Yes. AWP stands for Associated Writing Programs.

If you decide you want to teach in a college or university, this is the way to go. This is a generation that is looking for exchanges, and jobs, and affirmations that their studies in American poetry can be passed on to their students.

I don't think I ever called it "creative" writing. I mean, writing is writing. Mostly I was teaching/presenting examples of writing that I was already familiar with, that I thought "real." Like in a local class I did during these past six weeks. I just asked the members to write something every day: locate yourself, put the date and hour down, and then see what happens, what gets into your head. I gave them lots of examples from other writers, trying to make the act of writing easy and accessible without getting into these difficult questions about what "form" is this writing in? What is a poem? Fiction? What is creative nonfiction? What is this? What is that? Just write what's going on around you. Outside and inside.

You're trying to help them be poets?

Writers.

What was teaching at Naropa and New College like for you?

It was great. I could teach what I wanted. The students were responsive. I was always very careful not to tell them that what they were writing was "bad" or "good." The last class I gave at New College, before it closed, was a review of Japanese, Korean, Tibetan, and Chinese poetry. "Asian" poetry. When did it get translated into English or a "Western" language? The fact that we've only had translations for a couple of centuries. When did it start funneling through to the "Western mind"? And then, how did that travel to our American poets and readers?

Could we talk just a little bit, as a way of closing the circle, about what I think may have been one of the strongest efforts of your early career, the Odyssey poems, which you date between April 8 and December 1 of 1964. There, the primary focus is on Penelope, the stay-at-home wife. Your final entry in The Japan-India Journals *(aka* Strange Big Moon*) is dated February 3, the day you returned to San Francisco after you left Kyoto and your relationship with Gary Snyder. Do you think that was a sort of reprocessing in some ways of the experience of the relationship?*

Oh, yes. And then there were the suitors. And Spicer saying, "It has to do with your father." That's when I started calling my writing under the "Homer Dome." I metaphorically put Homer on my head and said, "Okay, let me write through Homer."

The forward-looking pieces are all about trying to find your home, too: the odyssey to get back there. And you hadn't found your home yet. That was still to come a few years down the road.

I went back again in the first poem in this new little book, *2012*:

WILD CURRENT IS BLOOMING PINK

You are in search of some simple way to reach your home
  but the old gods reach out with their stories and resentments

and so your journey will be troublesome
and frankly endless
for you will go on to meet people
who have never heard of you

Caught inland
by the outgoing long tide

Where you will find a place to plant some seeds
And tell your story all over

And give a bit of sacrifice
so those dead ones
can speak again.

Homer says that Ulysses is not going to die by the ocean; he's going to die without salt and away from the sea.

So that's February 18, 2012?

Yes, a year ago.

So it's still so much alive for you?

Well, it's a touchstone, isn't it? You know, there's nothing like finding a beautiful story from way back in history, like the Odyssey, in which so much happens. We're so lucky that it got written down. I'm sorry that we don't have our local Coast Miwok stories.

2013

They are constructing a craft
    solely of wood
at Waka-no-ura, fishing village,
    a jewel quite naturally
from the blue of the farm house tile roofs.

        found on the southern coast.

The women pull by hand long strings
          of seaweed across the shore

it dries
                  At the other end of the town
            the hull of the boat rises
above the smaller houses
A little prince of a boy in a white knit suit
    stands with the others in a group on the beach

Watching us go by, we are strange.
                    The women bend over
the seaweed, wakame, changing its face to the sun.

It is lonely

I must draw water from the well   75 buckets for the bath

I mix a drink — gin, fizz water, lemon juice, a spoonful
of strawberry jam

And place it in a champagne glass — it is hard work
to make the bath

And my winter clothes are dusty and should be put away

In storage.   Have I lost all values I wonder
the world is slippery to hold on to

When you begin to deny it.

Outside outside are the crickets and frogs in the rice fields

Large black butterflies like birds.

from *The Japan and India Journals*, 1960–1964

MARCH 2, 1962.

Moved across the Ganges to Swarg Ashram. Two rooms, for Peter & Allen, Gary & I. Afternoon walk down to sand and rock point of Ganges—white glittering sand. A few orange robes spread on rocks to dry. Everyone strips to undershorts, launders and bathes in the river.

Sadhus sitting in meditation, red eyes, matted hair up by the bridge. How can they sit so still says Allen. Gary changes last of my color film exposing by accident last pictures. Losing the following:

1. Portrait of Gary with wet hair, Allen behind in the Ganges.
2. Peter swimming, Allen & Gary bathing.
3. Gary meditating in sand, Allen standing on tall rock in background.
4. Allen, Peter, Gary sitting on bathing steps on Shivananda's side of river.
5. View from lodging across to other side of river from hill where we spent the first night at Rishikesh.
6. Gary in front of Agra Fort Pearl Mosque.

MARCH 3, 1962

Made Indian style tea on spirit burner—milk, tea, sugar, boiled together for us all. And rolls with jam and peanut butter. Studying maps. Always windy in the early morning here. And today cloudy and cool. Bird hops through the window looking for crumbs.

Reading Allen's article from *Second Coming*. "When the mode of music changes, the walls of the city shake."

Afternoon all of us on roof on hill. Ganges and small mountains behind us, on the Shivananda side. Swami Sri Lingam doing yoga asanas for us. The eyes, the mouth, being exercised. Great red meaty mouth.

Gary insists I eat yogurt and spills it over my mouth and sleeping bag. Leaves the cup outside and a dog eats it. A cat comes through the bars at night and knocks over a pail of it, comes back to lap it up.

Cows and bulls outside the door, one pins Allen to the gate. Peter pets them.

Chapter II from some book by Tim Leary at Harvard University Center for Research in Personality, who turns everyone onto mushroom pills. Pages peppered with words like: sweet loving guy, sweet new therapy, fine loving afternoon. He says he loves the poets but from the way he writes about them he turns them into unattractive foolish asses, drops just enough phrases through the mouths of others to show how he feels—no baths, big phone bill. Not very bright. Probably wants to write or be spiritual in big way—and envies Burroughs, Ginsberg—who he basically hates—covering it up with gooey admiration. 'Allen Ginsberg, Zen master politician.' Constantly harps on the poorer physical aspects of Allen—thin, glasses, white, stooped shoulders. 'Hung, like me, on doing good.'

MARCH 4, 1962.

The rest into Hardwar to see the beginning of Kumbh Mela. Terrific wind. Gloomy. Fuzzing of time. I could step back into Brentano's stock room.

Reading *Kim* all day between bouts of laundry. A grey heavy wind dries the clothes on the porch. Lugging buckets from the faucets at the pumps. Soaking the clothes for 30 minutes in the room and back to rinse and bringing back a fresh bucket for new laundry soaking. Sleeping bag liners, shawl, Gary's parka, and on.

Fruit salad when they return. I wear English man's long red sweater. Allen makes Peter in the next room.

MARCH 6, 1962.

Climbed the hill, Nealcant, behind the ashram, until noon to view Himalayas. One or two ice covered peaks. Some nearer foothills with snow. Green hills, farmer's house and land terraced down the side. They look like Nepali Hill folk.

MARCH 7

In Hardwar, walking up & down. The picture seller pulls the old beggar man's beard when he tries to help, and slaps his face.

MARCH 8

Traveling all night by train to Bareilly. At dawn, breakfast with two eggs. First non-vegetarian meal in two weeks. And on train and bus to Almora.

Crossing the river Ganges yesterday in morning boat with Jaipur peasants, they singing. The air and hills clear, river fast moving & muddy. Almost naked ascetic in Hardwar. Block printed Ram Ram cloth.

It's better to be a good man, than to be a yogi.

Four bridegrooms on the way. All young like adolescents. Bright umbrellas held over their heads, cheeks painted, beads hanging in front of their faces and tall bright colored hats, paper tinsel.

At the train station early, the bagpipe band of well trained and uniformed bandmen playing near a large beflagged tent set with cups and saucers waiting for a wedding party to arrive from Delhi.

Bus from Kuldani to Almora. Wreck after Raniket, government jeep has gone over the side of a cliff. A civilian riding illegally comes on back with us in the bus. His mouth and eye puffed and bloody. Everyone collects his baggage & dirty laundry. Broken suitcase. Peter gives first aid to soldier. His wrist broken. Head bloody. A truck takes him on to Raniket. Four or five people puking out the bus window all the way, including the little bridegroom, his father beside him. Sharp curves. Shining white mountain tops.

MARCH 14

Fever, brings cold. Made stew in and out of bed. Peter and Allen turn on with Morphine before dinner and no appetite. Peter has also taken Opium at 10 o'clock, before going to find his 12 rupee roast chicken was stewed in curry. He washed it off in the restaurant kitchen.

The next morning after buying Tibetan rug and hairy blanket we took the bus on to Kaumuni government rest lodge on ridge facing Trisul and surrounding ranges. Bask in sun all day facing the mountains, bundled all over, reading Gandhi's autobiography.

The chokidar makes us dinner. Kerosene lamps, fireplaces. Each room, 2 rupees a night. This morning on the way to Naini Tal, Peter and Allen sing rock and roll, blues.

Naini Tal has a lake, surrounded by high mountains, is a resort town with fancy Indians with transistor radios on trays and tweed jackets.

"Joanne Kyger, Poet, with her husband Gary Snyder holding umbrella, with priest from local temple connected with Gary's Daitoku-ji in Kyoto, home base for his Zen studies—we stayed over, wrote haikus in priest's family memento book, Joanne collected shiny pebbles, rainy day Sea of Japan, early 1963."

Photo and caption by Allen Ginsberg

Interview with Trevor Carolan, *Pacific Rim Review of Books*

Trevor Carolan: At some point you encountered the Pacific Northwest poetry contingent—Lew Welch, Gary Snyder, and Philip Whalen. Is it possible to quantify what their influence brought to Bay Area arts and letters?

Joanne Kyger: Perhaps in terms of work specific to location. The Six Gallery reading was a meeting, a collision of all the groups—the Pacific Northwest, San Francisco, Ginsberg/the Beats from New York. You had Michael McClure, Philip Lamantia, Rexroth as the M.C., Kerouac was there, Gary Snyder and Philip Whalen. Spicer was going to be part of it, but he was stuck back east, and Duncan was in Majorca or teaching at Black Mountain. It wasn't only the San Francisco people who were blessed by the alchemy of that historic event.

Somewhere in all of this there's the East West House that you were involved with . . .

Essentially, East West House was modeled after the Institute for Asian Studies when Alan Watts, among others, taught other like-minded people in Asian Studies. It closed and a group of students decided that they would start a communal house in which people who were interested could study Buddhist texts, Japanese, and go to Japan. Snyder had already gone there on his own. Gia-fu Feng, a translator from Chinese whose edition of the *Tao Te Ching* is still circulating, was living there too; also Claude Dahlenberg and Philip Whalen. Gia-fu went down to Big Sur and became part of the beginnings of the center at Esalen. I was there at the East West House in 1959 for a year and the house had been running for some years by then. They had sort of loosened their constraints and allowed women and other non-Japan-directed people to live there, but by then I was planning to go to Japan. There was an overflow of people from East West House and so they started something called Hyphen House, which was the hyphen between East and West. That was a few blocks away in what is now Japantown. Close by there was the Soto Buddhist temple where Shunryu Suzuki was invited to come and be the priest for the Japanese community in the Spring of 1959. He started zazen practice in the morning, open to everyone. He became the catalyst for beginning the Zen Center of San Francisco. I learned to sit there, during the year I spent at the East West House before going to Japan.

Before we head to Kyoto, can we get some sense of what the Pacific Northwest poets brought to arts and letters in San Francisco? A nature literacy? For example, attention to birdlife, to local flora is persistent throughout your writing . . .

When Lew Welch came he brought a particular kind of high energy. He also lived at East West House for a while. Philip Whalen's observations were always his own, from his own original and quirky mind. Snyder was more formal, using native American texts, his own work experiences, and explorations of the Pacific Northwest. I don't think it was until I moved to Bolinas in 1969 that I really entered into a close relationship with the land around me in my writing. About the birds who live here: to this day the quail are probably my closest neighbors. You get used to watching what's going on around you; you get to know what they're saying—the scrub jay announcing when someone is arriving. Bolinas is the location of the Point Reyes Bird Observatory, started back around 1965 and is a very well-known organization. They started banding birds and studying them and received enough endowments and patrons that they've begun studying birds farther afield—like the penguins in Antarctica. This is a great location for birds here, with a lagoon for blue herons and American egrets, many migrating ducks. Every year when the gold crown sparrows come down from the north, with the white-crowns—they have the Gold-Crown Festival. The gold-crowns have a very singular song, three descending notes. And they usually arrive right on the autumnal equinox.

So you're readying for Japan . . . What was the feel of things as you were gearing up to leave?

Don Allen edited the second edition of *Evergreen Review* which was called "The San Francisco Scene," because by then the San Francisco Renaissance had already mixed with this Beat thing and it was a cultural phenomenon. Something was happening. It had become a way of dressing, of semi-dropping out, of music and jazz with poetry, smoking grass—a cultural attitude that was a gigantic contrast against what the mainstream '50s were all about. Music was certainly a part of the North Beach scene—there was the Modern Jazz Quartet, Dave Brubeck, Paul Desmond. There were famous clubs to hear jazz. John Wieners gave me Olson's "Projective Verse" to read, and as a way of looking at writing and the page it was extremely important to me. Duncan had come to represent this attitude of the poet, of believing that you lived the life of the poet. Spicer was this cutting-edge sort of bullshit-detector all the time—whether a poem was true . . . you could tell if someone was faking it. "Poetry" poetry was out to lunch, so there was an astute sense of where you were coming from. These were valuable teachers.

And so Japan . . .

The four years I spent in Japan were spent more or less reading what was there in the British and American Cultural libraries. There was Cid Corman's *Origin* magazine, where I first read Lorine Niedecker . . . I was just practicing my own work—how to put words on the page, determining what's important; and when your emotion is going to take over, where to do your own internal editing before the work gets to the page. There were a number of figures writing or translating in the local community—Philip Yampolsky, Burton Watson, and the young poet Clayton Eshleman. Clayton was studying informally with Cid Corman—he was eager to find out things.

And then I also practiced "sitting." There were no books to read about Zen, in English then, and I was encouraged just to pay attention to breathing.

You returned to California . . .

After four years away I came back. Don Allen had visited and he wanted to publish my first book, *The Tapestry and the Web*. I found out that I was "okay" as a writer, whereas before I wasn't sure. Stan Persky started publishing something called *Open Space* magazine in 1964 which was very important. He put it out every month and ran things by Robin Blaser, Ebbe Borregaard, Lew Ellingham, etc., and everyone kind of turned everyone else on. I wrote a series of poems for him; Stan was still working in North Beach, so that was the cultural center.

Then there was the 1965 Poetry Conference in Berkeley and that essentially established certain poetry-political lines. Spicer died after that. I believe that's when Warren Tallman invited Robin to come up to Vancouver and Stan went up with him; George Stanley too, I think. Weren't they offered jobs? That made a big difference.

Did any other writers from that era have an influence upon you?

Albert Saijo. He published a little book about hiking in the Sierras, and then more recently *Outspeaks*, from Bamboo Ridge Press. It's one of my favorite books of poetry. He's so direct about what he does and says. He was there at the beginning of the psychedelic "revolution" in San Francisco. Lived at the East West House. Learned Zen meditation from Nyogen Senzaki in the late 1940s in Los Angeles. Very unaffected. He was a close friend of Lew Welch and Philip Whalen and Gary. A very modest fellow.

When you came back from Japan the Vietnam War was escalating. Did it affect the way you thought about your work?

Yes, but not overwhelmingly so. I lived in New York City, 1966–67, for a year and was part of a whole group there that became the Yippies. I worked doing some demonstrations with Keith Lampe (Ponderosa Pine), and "flower power" became one of our slogans. One of the Yippie group, Ed Sanders is responsible for trying to levitate the Pentagon, although Allen Ginsberg is often given credit for that. After the Be-In in San Francisco, we decided we should have something in Central Park and called it the "Spring Out." People smoked banana peels. But California was still more open about having a psychedelic revolution, dropping out, and generally being more politically confrontational.

During your years away you traveled India with Allen Ginsberg, Peter Orlovsky, and your then-husband, Gary Snyder. Regarding your experience there or in Japan, can you speak to how Buddhism, or dharma practice, might relate to your writing? You've mentioned at the symposium [The Beats in India] how one comes to pay attention to the moment, to details.

In India I became aware of this historical phenomenon called "Buddhism" which had 2,500 years of "moments." Seeing the origins of Buddhism in India, the Bodhi Tree, the Deer Park at Sarnath, Vulture's Peak, the great university of Nalanda, all in this cultural context of India, was an awakening. So "world history" became an awareness in my writing.

In Japan, since I didn't have a teacher, I learned the patience of sitting. That there isn't really anywhere to "go," although your mind surely wants to move like a rabbit.

You've also mentioned from your experience in India how you observed that when the Tibetans brought their diaspora down to India's historical Buddhist sites, they also brought their devotionalism . . .

Buddhism had not been practiced for centuries in India, although all the historical places related to the Buddha had been carefully tended to by British archeologists as part of a historical past. Then all of a sudden these places became full of the devotional energy of the Tibetans, with their friendly energy, and the power of the Vajrayana Himalayas with them.

You've been associated with Naropa University and its writing programs. Allen Ginsberg used to say, "Teach what you know—your own practice, own awareness . . ." Anything recommended for writers who may be coming up now?

It depends on what you know. I guess there could be a certain number of frisbee players teaching their practice. But how do you recognize or find what your awareness and practices are? Travel is certainly a way to see the world and your place in it. Understanding that you are in, a part of, a lineage of writers and teachers. That you didn't invent your "awareness," your practice—but are nonetheless individual in your own way and your understanding is unique.

Allen also used to say that the duty of the poet is to expand consciousness . . .

Yes, he said, after experiencing the power of yage, expand your consciousness so it encompasses your own death. Good advice. If you can do it. But don't you think we are already a part of that "expanded consciousness," that it has already happened?

Have you any response to the idea that Allen Ginsberg "walked out" at a certain critical moment from the Beat celebrity that ultimately killed Jack Kerouac? In '62 Allen dropped off the radar and ended up traveling in India, part of it with you and your then-husband . . .

After reading *Kaddish* at the San Francisco Poetry Center, he traveled to South America for six months, by himself, initially to take part in a reading with Lawrence Ferlinghetti in Chile, and then went on to travel in South America on the yage trail. He took it eight times, altogether, and then he decided he needed a teacher, which he thought he could find in India. He probably dropped out of sight from the heightened publicity surrounding the Beat Generation at that time, but returned from his travels and helped facilitate the counterculture revolution in the early '60s. Also he never really drank alcohol, so didn't have Kerouac's problems in that regard.

In the various individually published accounts of that journey there are points of subtle (and sometimes not so subtle) discrimination between how some group experiences are reported by Allen, Gary, and yourself . . . Anything about your own personal approach in this?

My journals were written on the spot. Gary's were written after he returned, as a letter. And Allen's were edited. Being the sole woman on the trip, there were of course differences, in the physicalities of travel. But that would be true of any trip.

After meeting with a youthful Dalai Lama, you come away and write in your journal that Allen "actually believes he knows it all, but just wishes he felt better about it . . ."

A slightly sarcastic tone, but true, I think.

*You've already got one other new collection of poetry out following your Collected—*Not Veracruz *(Libellum). What's your sense of the poetic grounding in this mature work?*

Grounding? Hopefully, the simpler, the better.

2007

Memories of Kerouac

I am living at the East West House on California Street during 1959, and Jack Kerouac comes to town with the painter Al Leslie for the showing of Robert Frank's & his movie, *Pull My Daisy*.

The whole cast consisted of amateurs—Ginsberg and Orlovsky as themselves, Larry Rivers as Neal, Corso as Jack, Richard Bellamy as the Bishop, Dave Amram as a cowboy. Carolyn played by actress Delphine Seyrig.

Six weeks of shooting. Jack gets banned from set for bringing in the worst of the Bowery bums to Al Leslie's studio where the film was being shot. Film runs 90 minutes. Jack is supposed to lip synch but sounds like stage manager in *Our Town*.

Film reduced to 29 minutes, Jack improvises a new narration at Jerry Newman's studio while watching the film and listening on earphones to Amram play jazz. He hadn't slept in a day and a half but was keyed up. Al Leslie has Jack repeat performance two more times, one in a Chinese accent, and additional narration in French describing the story as if it were taking place in Lowell. The emphasis in PULL MY DAISY upon the environment of a fifties New York tenement heightens the impact of the basic human situation the film portrays. The three versions are cut together. Film becomes honored as new wave and one of the first underground films. November 16 '59 he flys to LA to be on the Steve Allen show in his new tweed jacket, which he is buried in ten years later.

He reads on the show, with the last page of *Visions of Cody* taped inside *On the Road*. He meets up with Al Leslie there. Sees rushes of *The Subterraneans*. Collects 2,000 dollars from Steve Allen Show, and 12,000 balance on *The Subs*, sends it to his mother, and lived off Leslie all the way to San Francisco. They stay at the Hyphen House, the dash between East West House of which it was an extension. He meets Jay Blaise, Lew Welch, Albert Saijo. Lew is in high energy excitement to see him.

Lew takes them to the Zoo where they drink Pernod and Jack comes back to the East West House and lays on the kitchen floor. Late night discussion at the Hyphen House. They are going to fix Jack up with a girl. Jay knows this girl. She's in such bad shape she'll fuck anyone. She has a glass of whiskey by her bed. Just waiting for Jay to call. She'll do it. What a heartless use of women! I throw a gallon of wine at Jay. It breaks on the wall and a flying piece of glass cuts him over the eyebrow. Lew Welch jumps up and down screaming, You Spoil Everything. Albert and Lew and Jack take off the next day for New York, writing Haikus along the way. (*Trip Trap*, published by Don Allen's Grey Fox Press in 1973.)

So what is it about Kerouac's influence. His terrific use of words, bubbling away. His wonderful tone. The great ability to tell a story. Especially about friends I knew. The excitement of the truth, of the times. The Beat Generation Energy.

October 15, 1991

Jan. 9, 1960

Dear Joanne Elizabeth,

I had hoped to be able to come to San Francisco to watch you sail away on that boat, but Willy won't run anymore and I don't even have enough money for anything at all (even).

Therefore I will say goodbye and wish you well by means of this (very) letter which you are, I trust, now reading.

Goodbye. Best wishes. I wish I had a charm or something to give as token of my esteem.

You must meditate all the way to Japan, practice those funny little bows, and keep your boots greased. You must also practice exactly what to say when you meet Mdme. Sasaki.

I hope you love Gary as much as he seems to love you (whatever that means -- I confess to being entirely without understanding of anything connected with the cohabitation of men and women, though I have from time to time felt emotions something like those described ((wrongly I'm convinced)) in novels great and mean, only to become confused when the parrying starts. It is like standing there with a tennis racket and discovering that the other player is equipped with a bowling ball). (or a turtle.)

Still I have seen pairs which get along fine, and when one sees this (as I did recently on that Sausalito houseboat) it is strange and wonderful. It is probably the best of all that is.

I bless you with my little beach shell. (smack!)

This letter is written on a teletype roll as per Jack's writing theory. I am writing well on my novel -- about 10 feet per day. I have learned two things: (1) To write a long prose work it is necessary, as Stein said, to "wait around all day for the time you will write." You just hang around patiently, washing dishes, baking hams, or just staring, and suddenly there you are walking, trancelike, toward the typewriter and soon you have dropped right into it and don't come up for several hours. The book begins to become a real life which you look forward to returning to each day. It is not hard work, but it is not possible to do it if you have anything else <u>at all</u> to do. (2) Novels must be written on long rolls of teletype paper, because there is something absolutely wrong with writing a long continuous narrative on short discontinuous pieces of paper.

I am lonely and depressed except when deeply writing, but see as in the most lucid sort of vision that never again will my lonliness render me helpless as it has so often in the past. The vision I have shows me that my only task from here on out is to finally accept the fact that I will never know the steady daily love of a wife, and I will never have any money. However, the vision also tells me I will have, to a great degree, everything else.

Several nights ago the clearest message I ever received from my muse went (almost audibly):

> First you must love your body, in games,
> in wild places, in bodies of others.
>
> Then you must enter the world of men and
> learn all worldly ways. You must sicken.
>
> You must then return to your Mother and
> notice how quiet the house is.
>
> Then ~~you~~ return to the world that is
> not Man
>
> that you may finally walk in the
> world of Man, speaking.

Then our old brass clock that has been in our home since the year one, struck. Bong Bong Bong!

Bong?

yr-very-best-frin-in-the-whol-worl

Lew

Buzz Time

I come back to San Francisco in January of 1964, after four years of living in Kyoto, Japan. It's fantastic, four dimensional, I can understand what is being said, everyone speaks English, the Beatles in the air for the first time, a great colorful buzz.

And there is to be a gallery called Buzz. Run by Paul Alexander, Bill Brodecky (Moore), and Larry Fagin. I have just met Larry Fagin at Gino & Carlo's Bar in North Beach. He says, I heard you were in town, and I planned to welcome you with a black ink-filled water pistol. Very Dada.

There is a new order of my writing friends. The poets have just been given a new magazine: Stan Persky is to publish OPEN SPACE once a month for the next year, actually 15 issues in all come out.

A specific list of writers and artists are invited and anything they submit will be published—Robin Blaser, Robert Duncan, Helen Adam, myself, George Stanley, Ebbe Borregaard, Harold Dull, Lew Ellingham, Jack Spicer. And artists, Bill McNeill, Bill Wheeler, Bill Brodecky, Harry Jacobus, Robert Duncan, Helen Adam, Fran Herndon, Ken Botto, Tom Field, Paul Alexander. These artists, along with Nemi Frost became part of the Buzz Gallery Group.

I have always thought painters have much more glamour in the world than writers. Something more tangible from their creations: self confident and casual. Something beautiful you can see on a wall.

I first meet Paul Alexander and Tom Field in 1958 inside the fascinating pace of North Beach. They have come from the famous Black Mountain College in North Carolina, and were originally from Fort Wayne, Indiana, where they had known each other since grade school.

My first meeting with Paul remains like a snap shot vision. He's in one of the little studios in the famous, and now torn down, Monkey Block near North Beach. Tom Field has taken me to visit—"I want you to meet an old friend of mine." It's fall 1958. I'm wearing a smart walking cast recovering from a broken ankle. They both have beautiful gracious manners, and great humor. Paul has a particular wonderful laugh. He is soft spoken, hospitable, warm. He gives detailed, precisely worded, original twists to his stories. His small abode looks like a tiny palace—like his later places. Books, pottery, plants, tiny treasures, paintings, drawings, sculpture. There is always excellent talk at the slow dinners. The table becomes the world.

When Paul draws, it is with an intimate line, quick, moving, a body, a horizon. There are many beautiful drawings and watercolors, paintings of gleaming, creamy colors.

Tom Field is such a solicitous person, cooking, taking care of his friends. A merchant seaman he is in and out of town. His paintings use big amazing brush strokes. He wins the top award from the San Francisco Museum of Modern Art Annual in 1962. His drawings quick and whimsical.

Neither Paul or Tom are self promoters in a larger art world. When they reside at Buzz it is always a great social occasion, like visiting the artist "at home" in a grand drawing room.

Bill McNeill and Ernie Edwards live along the balcony next door to Buzz Gallery.

Bill, originally from North Carolina, also attends Black Mountain College before he comes to San Francisco. Very quick and multitalented, he is searching for a "direction." I first meet him in The Place in North Beach in 1958 where he tells me about his interest in Zen Buddhism and about this teacher he has found who has just come from Japan. His name is Shunryu Suzuki and this is the beginning of the San Francisco Zen Center. I go with Bill to meet Suzuki because I am interested in Japan and Zen too.

After studying for a year and a half with Suzuki, Bill sails to Japan and becomes ordained as a monk. A few months later, feeling isolated, Bill moves to Kyoto, where I run into him again. He is teaching English to Japanese business men and telling tales of covering sliding paper doors with flashy black sumi strokes. He speaks Japanese with a very southern accent. Finally he decides he's had enough of Zen and Japan and returns to San Francisco in late 1961.

After Bill returns from Japan he collaborates with the poet Helen Adam on an experimental movie called *Daydream of Darkness*. Dramatic, darkly magical, very San Francisco.

Bill is always consumed with his enthusiasm of the moment, and with his charismatic personality "spreads the word," including those around him in his projects. During the Buzz years Bill works on his second movie. The plot, at least for me, is very confusing. At one point I find myself playing a mini-role down in Monterey Bay, early one Sunday morning. I'm on a cold rocky beach, decked out in a green taffeta tunic welcoming a glistening black rubber clad scuba diver as he emerges from the water. It's all quite uncomfortable. What does it mean, is it mythological? I don't think the film was ever completely finished but there were lots of screening parties and often shown "in progress" at grand social occasions during the Buzz years.

Bill is also great at cultivating group watercolors around his round table—goldfish in a bowl, iris, flowers in season. We were all busy painting away at our versions of what we saw. Bill's line is quick, stylish, sumilike.

His poppies on a gold leaf Japanese style folding screen was a real tour-de-force and sold for quite a bit of money—which was unusual and refreshing. It only showed for a short time at Buzz, all by itself in the gallery, before the owner picked it up.

2002

Buzz Gallery, 1965. Nemi Frost's painting show. Left to right: Ernie Edwards, Bill Brodecky Moore, Paul Alexander, Joanne Kyger, Jack Boyce, Nemi Frost (foreground). Photo by Jim Hatch.

In July

Geraniums

Taking a walk in the morning
        the warm mist like rain

Jack picked a nasturtium about 7

        Quiet lake with water lilies
    no one harms anything that comes down there

the family comes with smiles
    thru the large luxurious rooms of the house
scattered thru in white clothing like flowers
        take your time, take your time

this is a guest house where all are taken care of

the great and good sun comes out, the sun is a star

She finished up the web, it had to do with her father she said
using it to keep them away for many years, tricking them.
Hermes came to get the dead suitors.
Persephone really died every year
to go down there was difficult a large dark house
and ghost groves on either side one of white. They called her terrible

It has been difficult to write this. One day
I walked around the block, it was grey, and whatever was green on the lawns was clear
the flower pots on the back porch, the neighbor's steps to the second floor
I could have watched for a long time,
why they must go to war I can't decide

to settle fear. we were all born
They are coming towards the house someone calls to Odysseus
and he is that great fighter
having a guide, a female presence who pulls her own self into battle also
A great struggle in Persephone's field of poppies
a broken sprig of geranium
It is not for me to control she calls
the loud men rising towards each other, great turmoils that pull
through all of you, I give you style in battle
the final control is man
Zeus calls halt.
takes all this nature from running riot, the thundering push
of green buds, leaves, grass, roaring
in the sky filling it with birds, the clouds
closing down, mountains rocking, sinks

a flaming bolt, the control takes peace

over an ordered landscape, it is clear
all confusion gone, and nodding their heads wondered where they had gone.

12.1.64

Interview with Linda Russo, *Jacket*

PHOTOGRAPHS BY JOANNE KYGER, 1958

Linda Russo: I want to back up a little bit, to something you'd mentioned earlier—that the so-called Beat Movement was more of a "newspaper phenomenon" than a "literary phenomenon."

Joanne Kyger: What did I say, more of "a cultural media phenomenon" than a "literary phenomenon." But I think that's true of a lot of literary movements. Writers are associated with one another, then they get a name or a handle on them afterwards, like the "Objectivists."

The "Beat" origin myth has several stages, according to Ginsberg, but he gives primacy to Kerouac in conversation with John Clellon Holmes. But what you're saying suggests that the term "Beat" didn't so much work to establish an aesthetic affinity between writers as to shape it and announce it to others—non-writers—as in a cosmetic production.

Allen was a person who liked to grandstand. The writers he loved and was close to, he'd work very hard to get them published. I think he was as responsible as anyone else for turning it into a group of writers: here's Gary Snyder's poem, here's Philip Whalen's, here's Kerouac, here's Corso . . .

And then there's the idea that the beat phenomena came from New York versus the idea that there was already something happening in the Bay Area when the Beats showed up.

It was the Berkeley Renaissance, a group of writers around Robert Duncan, Jack Spicer, James Broughton, and Robin Blaser that brought all those people together, through the '40s they had an established literary, cultural closeness. Then in San Francisco during the '50s there were happenings with jazz and poetry, Ferlinghetti, Rexroth. Before *Howl* was published, the Six Gallery reading . . . but I don't think they were identified as beat writers at that moment, 1955–56. The Six Gallery sets off this group of writers, many of them met each other for the first time, Ginsberg meets Gary Snyder, Michael McClure.

And the Philips: Whalen and Lamantia.

[Whalen had] come down from Oregon. He and Gary were old roommates up at Reed College. This sparked a kind of energy. Later it was the publication of *On the Road*. It became a media phenome-

Robert Duncan, Ebbe Borregaard, Jack Spicer

non—the characters in it, and in the *Dharma Bums* became celebrities, and *Howl* being censored brought this more into the forefront, the laid back lifestyle of the "beatnik," a term coined by Herb Caen, became a cultural phenomenon: the guy in the sandals, the bongo drums, beret, poetry and jazz, and this was opposed to the establishment.

There's a more recent anthology, A Different Beat: Writing by Women of the Beat Generation*, and yet again we have this same positioning of women who weren't "beat" necessarily.*

Lenore Kandel is early '60s . . . I think it's a way to put a bunch of women together that didn't personally consider themselves beat writers. "Beat" has just become a cultural word now.

There's two definitions: "of the Beat generation," which is how these anthologies choose to talk about women who bear signs of being, contemporaneously or consequently, under the influence of beat aesthetics, and "Women who were Beats," as in women who wrote, lived in, and actively developed that milieu. Are there any women you would put in the latter category?

How do you define what a "Beat writer" is?

Well, that's the problem. There's the association of "women of the beat generation," which is a retrospective grouping. You get little sense of what it means, in terms of the poetry and the poetics that a group produces, to be associated with that group. Are associations aesthetic only? In terms of life- and writing-style?

So if we say it's the women that were non-academics of the '50s . . .

And that knocks out one of Brenda Knight's primary "Precursors," Josephine Miles, and raises questions about Denise Levertov's inclusion in her anthology, Women of the Beat Generation. *The problem with anthologies is that any sense of real, material circumstance falls away, and there's this false aesthetic transcendence.*

I guess it's a way to access certain writers. It's useful to be part of the group, because then you can get a handle on the group of the moment in a book together. Someone like ruth weiss, I remember her coffeehouse readings from the '50s. Janine Pommy Vega, she comes along a little later but so did I.

Right—and there's a parallel here between establishing aesthetic affinity—that moment of putting a book together, recognizing a group as a group—and cosmetic production—the packaging of women, in this case, as products of the beat. But how many of these women who are gathered under this grouping would select themselves to be of that movement?

Hettie Jones certainly feels herself to be part of that movement, I've heard her speak of that.

She co-edited the very important little magazine Yugen *with the then-LeRoi Jones. Well actually she typed all of the issues, she's written explicitly of that—of the significance of that, along with paying for paper, offset printing, arranging for distribution, etc.—to the production of the magazine.*

And Joyce Johnson . . .

There's Joyce Johnson, writing of her life with Kerouac in Minor Characters. *Joan Kerouac wrote an article for* Esquire *called "Jack Kerouac is a sleazebag" or something like that. One wonders why we glorify the beat era as fertile for women writers at all, except to* somehow *define them . . .*

Jan Kerouac, associated by proximity and style . . .

And genealogy. But that's not an identification you would make?

It's not useful to me. And also the beat writers at the time read at the Coffee Gallery, the Bread and Wine Mission. There's still *Beatitude* that comes out, which was really a particularly politically inspired forum, but not very good poetry. My practice of writing was a lot stricter, coming from the energy of Spicer, and someone like Robert Duncan who was opposed to the tendency of Beat popular poetry writing—to let it all dribble out . . .

Harold Dull, Joanne Kyger, and George Stanley

Would you compare it to the Poetry Slam? Very populist, people hanging out in bars, reading poetry to each other?

Yes.

Whereas, from what I know about the Magic Workshop and the Sunday Meetings at the Dunns' etc. it was more focused on poetry as a structure, on the line, on words. It seems to be very different than an expressive / excessive approach to poetry. You have a poem in Just Space *where you talk about knowing the architecture of your lineage. Could you read it, and talk a little bit about it?*

Well, it's pretty straightforward (reads):

You know when you write poetry you find
the architecture of your lineage your teachers
like Robert Duncan for me gave me some glue for the heart
Beats which gave confidence
and competition
to the Images of Perfection

. . . or as dinner approaches I become hasty
do I mean PERFECTION?

What was it about the Beats which gave confidence?

Heart Beat—wasn't that the name of that book by Carolyn Cassady, about her many encounters with Kerouac? Ginsberg's own sense of heart, of the family of poetry, although he was a terrible misogynist later, some of the women that he trusted became acceptable to him.

What about "perfection"?

I don't know what we mean by that—"images of perfection." I'm not sure what perfection means, obviously. Could you make a perfect dinner? What's perfect?

What's interesting is the competition. Because that would imply an engagement with something—a politics, a person, an aesthetic—that you could argue with, that you might perhaps call "Beat" to set it aside from yourself.

Beat was a period of history and until very recently nobody tried to make that a working historical phenomenon. Allen always was able to talk about his own history. Kerouac died in '69 and that ended a certain era. He certainly was the main writer of that time, the *On the Road* phenomenon—the reprinting of his books in the last five or six years since the death of his wife, all his books were able to be reprinted—so people got interested again. Making up a literary history is the phenomenon of looking back and trying to make a picture of a puzzle. So trying to ask someone *now* "what did you feel like then"—I didn't think about it in that way, I thought about it as a practice of my own writing that I was interested in, and certainly a lot of the ideas that came through the quote "beat generation"—I didn't call them the "beat generation." Gary Snyder's idea of opening Pacific Rim ideas, but there wasn't a

Pacific Rim that anybody talked about then. A lot of it was Allen's idea of expanding consciousness, opening up the cultural avenues of what a writer can see and articulate, and maybe nobody had articulated this before, or seen this, or done this before. The whole Judeo-Christian world was not enough culturally . . . how do you see yourself, not as a religious idealist, but what are the acculturating generosities of Buddhism? What is the practice of looking at your mind? And it's certainly on the heels of that, taking LSD. That was a huge cultural phenomenon based in some of the ideals of dropping out, or like Gary and the "rucksack revolution." If you want to be a writer, you don't have to be in the academy. What you want to do is make enough money at an ordinary job so you can do your own writing, that your friends are your audience, that you don't have to be in *Kenyon Review*. There is a life you can make as a writer that doesn't have to do with the academic tradition which was prevalent then. So it was the beginning of a kind of dropping out.

> *In talking about the Beat generation maybe the stress should be on the idea of* generation. *What I hear you talking about mostly are the ideas that were beginning to circulate about consciousness, about approaching poetry in a different way, about approaching religion in a different way. The concept of "generation" is more important than a particular, "beat," identity. Would that be a helpful way to think about it?*

Maybe. I don't think people think about it, when you're leading your life, are you thinking about "thinking" new ideas? You're thinking about getting along, and trying to find a way to get your poetry out there, to read it to each other. But you're somewhat in an academic tradition right now in Buffalo, but I think, to veer away from trying to generalize, from trying to make a point of an entire generation, to try and particularize people's lives and pasts would be more useful for myself.

1997

Letter From Paris

JOANNE KYGER AND LARRY FAGIN

19 AVRIL 1966

To think of Dave Haselwood in Paris screw both your eyes up so the veins pop out on our brow and we'll see.

By and by we are here in Paris the Athens of France. Joanne Elizabeth Kyger-Boyce John Phillip Boyce Lawrence Edward Henry Fagin Micasar Ja Origine Algerie Pommes de Frescomint Collins French Gem Howdy Do. For a second we thought Dave Haselwood more than human anyhow. Philip Lamantia is Nowhere To Be Seen. And now the news with Santa Barbara's Very Own Gibson Girl JEK-B:

Well, Kids, let me give you some of the *low down*. Hems are *short*. Color is *in*. John Ashbery is in New York, and not around the corner snubbing us as I thought. We are not speaking to Gregory Corso in Paris because we do not think he would speak to us. Raymond Duncan is down the street, but he is too *old*. Thomas Clark would not meet us at Deux Magots because of personal appearance reasons but he met us next door at the Cafe Flor where Lawrence chug-a-lugged three cocoas in a row and ran up a terrible *bill*.

Well, Dave, Paris is really Paris it even smells like it of course there's A Drugstore here but never you mind. Jean Phillippe is 2 heures late from Amexco so we're debating on buzzing up la police just in case. The sun just broke through. Huzzah. Just get a load of Joanne seated in the sunlit window like an upsidedown odalisque in an ad for Coty . . . fondulac! it's refreshing! What do you think, Dave, should we go to a vernissage uninvited tonight? Is the only thing wrong is your feet get tired in Paris the New York of France. We're writing novels just like everybody else. We've *got* to. I'm reading a dirty book called Busy Bodies. (cut–pan to:

Well! I must admit that I am a bit confused about my novel, that is to say, after I move around inside it enough, I forget that there is an *outside*, that one simply must go to in order to get refreshed and tidied up and titillated, without of course not losing the track of hemlines and haircuts etc. And one must never allow oneself to become *suspicious* in this state. We lay with a great deal of aplomb on the red velvet seats in the Grande Salon in the Louvre last Sunday and looked at Napoleon crowning Josephine in the Notre Dame, and Gericault's RAFT which is Larry's very favorite painting in the entire existing galaxies until he goes into the next room and sees another one, and Courbet's Gallery painting, and Delacroix's Harem scene with every one tumbling about into horse's mouth's and bedspreads and daggers and Rome burning in the background etc. I am going now to the window to see if the Seine is being dragged out for John Philip and/or also he may come out of a vegetable shop, or I shall wait until five cars pass that corner and I eat five dates and Then he will be here.

Don't beautify your mistakes I always say.

A terrible abstraction is setting in sometimes. It listens in on *my* novel and doesn't like what it hears, after all it's a novel like everybody else's novel, that is the idea. (if it gets *in* it we call it "causal control" or une chausee blanc. I am trying for a new Vie de Boehme with oomph. Otherwise the rest of the folks are translating Max Jacob's Dice Cup, eg.

THE AUDOMETER

It is composed of a rubber tube with an immobile alidad running around its edges and a sort of photographic device in the middle. The audometer was made for speaking to a person present without being heard by others. It is also used to send pills to someone sick in bed without bothering him.

—trans. Ron Padgett

They carried musk and grenadine on Gericault's raft. If it's badly drawn (receding shinbones) as Joanne says, it's only because it is. Of course, this is a Very French letter, and they kissed her hand and fainted dead away. We have not seen the dear dead bones of Napoleon in his grave yet, but Larry says that one should always have at least one miniature of him in one's house. It is a bit hard to suppose what Jack would say as he has not yet arrived. I have almost figured out, now, what direction he will come from, or be borne from.

Well so much for that. We are not at all sure if Ron Padgett would like us to come by, and whereas we are mildly sure George Tysh would not mind, do you think he would give us Champagne? even though '66 is not a terribly good year? and he has a Hungarian girl friend? Well, alas I cook on an alcohol stove in the bidet and our suitcase has been lost for three weeks. Jack has gone after it and he will also be lost for three weeks or a taxi cab got him. I am reading Jack London's *Jerry of the Islands* which is all about a dog. Sigh, and they kissed her hand and fainted dead away and she also fainted dead away, and the whole room breathed inaudibly and peacefully. Merci.

DESSINS

Paris has welcomed us with open arms in short sleeves. The red hair of his forearms are erectable so difficult a time he is having choosing the prettiest of the three. Okay, I want radishes, brown pears, camembert, vin ordinaire, petit pain, peach melbe, fresco-mints, raisins and almonds and I want them on a brand new mahogony tric-trac table with a zinc top. Timeless and bottomless. Joanne is beautiful in her Sassoon hair, her hands flutter away to another arrondisement where the collective head of the congress of young French poets has been waiting for a pat. Helas, it's raining. Where is Jack? Ou est Jacques? Qui est mois? Michael McClure ne existe pas. They've scrubbed all the public bldgs. clean. You would still recognize it no less than your own home town. Caesar's Men are pretty in a small jar of water on the mantle.

Some pretty final decisions have been made around here. If Jack does not come back he is sulking because there is no peanut butter in France. We are not going to mention him again unless you read about it in the newspapers.

Well, the rain has stopped and we shall make no more idiotic references to that again. The coffee is hot and we are going to drink it. The floor is firm the room has a ceiling. We have not seen Jean Paul Sarte or Jean Paul Belmondo and they have not changed our sheets for two weeks. Yesterday they gave us a towel though. We thought we were going to a pretty nice French Restaurant but Larry said it was a Turkish restaurant.

I *knew* it was a Greek restaurant, but only because I was told for I am a hick. We are thinking of the things we'd make you do if you were only here. Hey, Dave, are you an existentialist? I wonder if I am because of the way I think, burning crosses. The squat red clock says cockadoodle 3:45 skidoo so we're on our way but before we go:

LARRY: I don't miss San Francisco.

JOANNE: I'm not committing myself.

LARRY: Do you think you're pretty hot stuff?

JOANNE: I think I'm middle-age stuff.

LARRY: Does Dave Haselwood like us?

JOANNE: Dave Haselwood has an appreciative fond of us.

LARRY: Where do we want to go now?

JOANNE: Let's just take a walk or something.

LARRY: Paris is for the very young.

JOANNE: There must be some interesting middle-aged people around.

LARRY: Give your love to Dave Haselwood.

JOANNE: Yes I'm giving my fondest regards to Dave Haselwood.

I TOLD YOU BILL BROWN IS OK. HOPE FOR THE BEST.

Dear Joanne, I just signed giant contract papers with James Koller & Wm Jovanovich, of Harcourt, Brace & World {NYC} for a hardcover & "quality paperback" book of "Selected Poems by PW" Jim should be in NYC right about now, to finish executing the rest of the papers & arranging arrangements with Corinth Books {about reprinting part or all of LIKE I SAY} When the papers are signed I'm supposed to get $1000. I shall come to San Francisco, I think, about 1st November to work with Jim on preparing the ms. which must be in NYC before 1st January 1968 — & they promise to publish before 1st January 1969. And I'm applying again for a Guggenheim Fellowship — in order to really get to India &c. I guess I can't make it right this minute. Maybe next year. YES, I also want to live in woods while I'm in America. Also big Buddhist takes via psilocybin & LSD, yes. "Absolutely." as Olson says. October 20 is my birthday but I guess I can spare it. Only exorcisms I know are the "Dharani against disaster" {in THE WOODEN FISH, & in Suzuki's MANUAL OF ZEN} and the long prayers in the appendix to the TIBETAN BOOK OF THE DEAD. The Prajnaparamitahridaya Mantram is also a spell against all demons &c. NYC as a "center" went to pot when the Living Theater was busted... then Frank O'Hara died, &

that really finished it. Aram Saroyan lives in Massachusetts ... Jefferson Airplane is in San Francisco. New York may make a come-back later. But like all cities, they have this drive on to throw out the poor people — no lofts, no slums, & noplace for the scholar, the musician, painter or poet. So all of us have got to figure out how to stay alive in the country. I'm very scared by the official reaction to the riots in America — the cops & the government are really scared, & so are all property owners. If <u>they</u> get scared enough, there'll be a fascist revolution in U.S.A. As for poetry, I expect you're just "wrung out" temporarily, after having finished so much work. How well do you know Chaucer? Shakespeare & his contemporaries? The Greek lyric poets? Medieval European stuff? Dante? Sanskrit poetry newly translated? David Hawkes translation of the Ch'u Tsu? IT AIN'T DEAD. Love.

Phil

はじめに ここを おる First fold here

PAR AVION 航空郵便

AEROGRAMME

NIPPON 50

ams 8/14

Mrs. Joanne Boyce
36 Greene Street
New York City, N.Y. 10013
U.S.A.

つぎに ここを おる Second fold here

差出人住所氏名
Sender's name and address Philip Whalen c/o Kitamura
73 Higashikubota-cho, Kita-Shirakawa,
Sakyo-ku, Kyoto JAPAN

この郵便物にはなにも入れたりはりつけたりすることができません
Nothing may be contained in or attached to this letter.

T/O

To open cut here

In 1968, Joanne completed a residency at the first year of the National Center for Experimental Television in San Francisco (NCET). Collaborative videos and films, using synchronized psychedelic visuals, sound loops, and feedback were created between poets, painters, musicians, and filmmakers and eventually shown on public television (KQED). The producer behind the project, Brice Howard, also worked on video vignettes with Charles Olson and Robert Creeley. Joanne's project was *Descartes*, an eleven-minute black and white video based on her poem "Descartes and the Splendor Of—A Real Drama of Everyday Life. In Six Parts." Her principal collaborators were filmmaker Loren Sears and musician Richard Felciano.

Letter from Charles Olson (1968)

28 Fort Square Gloucester
September 27th
(Saturday)
LXVIII

Dear Joan—

That honored me, to have your delicious Script, And your letter—- and don't mind at all I have been delayed in telling you. (For one thing just about the day—in fact THE day by god you wrote the letter enclosing it I met this 42 yr old Swedish woman (come to see me from there)—and once more knew the delights. . . . I mean still do know the feeling again of having fallen in love. Yes: Exactly August 7 (in the AM). Crazy, woman——and I was going to say to you that because of the Mother God therein, you had in fact written new rules for a new ANCIENT RITE! By God! I must say at least she's still like-as she always was, and will be -Venus?

Ok. and happy as hell to have all your news. Miss you both— and as of the project still talk & talk and the crazy beautiful death's head pendant (and do in fact think the only way to avoid this black jelly is to have only such a film as that (plus actually also that possibility of the traveling set going over the ground looking for, or finding finally it's one drink of water) exposed for the two full years—and nothing else unless the equivalents (have THAT confidence in Loren—and who did the traveling television set?

But of course which brings me back to you as premier poetissima of the Medium. Wow. (I just do believe that. no put on. You are the -Star.

So please give the KQUED gang my best (with Loren, privately, give the special pinch —-and you both keep my love, here? Even though I'd be happy too to be remembered to your own list of the loved and distracting people.

From O (over
here Charles

(Back of envelope): Love and hope you are a thousand times more wonderful and happy as I believe to you have to be! Being so much, like you!

Joanne—Put your address on the inside of things: envelopes are such beautiful things to write on!

Olson is writing Joanne in response to her script for Descartes *as well as thinking back on his own experience performing at NCET. Olson's video was based on a piece from the final pages of* The Maximus Poems *beginning, "Wholly absorbed / into my own conduits to / some inner nature or subterranean lake . . ." Olson was clearly taken with Joanne's appropriation and expansion of Descartes's* Discourse on the Method *(1637), in particular her changing the philosopher's voice from male to female. In an essay titled* Joanne Kyger "Descartes and the Splendor Of": Bridging Dualisms through Collaboration and Experimentation, *Jane Falk writes, "Kyger's most radical move is to feminize Descartes, shown dramatically in her video production. She provides the voice-over, simultaneously narrating and acting out her poem, as she takes on the role of both the contemporary woman / Descartes and Mother God / God. Her powerful and hieratic female voice is an important and effective part of her parody."*

PART VI

The difficulties of trusting and using your own mind.
The *I* that is the Pivot, must not wobble, in the name of the established compendium of minds.
MOTHER GOD has created all, and I found this from MY OWN MIND,
whence reside the germs of all truth.
And from her, THE FIRST CAUSE, comes the sun and the moon and the stars, Earth, water, air, fire, minerals, porridge.
                                                  And from here,
I may explain all the objects brought to my senses. And ALL THE
RESULTS WHICH I HAVE DEEMED IMPORTANT I HAVE
BROUGHT TO YOU, NOT FOR MY PRIVATE USE but for ANY VALUE
THEY MAY HAVE TO THOSE AFTER ME; for our CARES OUGHT
TO EXTEND BEYOND THE PRESENT.
                    But it is the proof of my own mind's abilities,
any ONE MIND'S ABILITIES THAT MY UNDERTAKING DRAWS
TO PROOF. ONE CANNOT SO WELL LEARN A THING WHEN
IT HAS BEEN LEARNED FROM ANOTHER, AS WHEN ONE HAS
DISCOVERED IT HIMSELF.

Mother God in the Castle, of Heaven.

Cover of *Joanne*, Angel Hair Books (1970), photo by Bill Berkson

UNDER THE GREEN LIGHT

You see when the new spirit came along
  it had to get on top
  of the old spirits.
So the old spirits
  were pushed underground
  by the weight.
    And they're only dark
  when seen from the perspective
of light, because the new spirit
  saw them as raw
  untidy, out of order,
and they only moved at night
  and tried to be out of sight
forgotten in this dusty corner.
    Oh eeek get that spider
out of here
  And under the ground in seed holes
  and hanging from trees upside down
    and lost souls
  who don't know which
    way to go, dark or light
    good or bad
      Say oh leader of the lost
    promise me the company
of the dark, oh the passing
      smell, the shimmer
    oh it grows like a snake

moves like the strongest
most beautiful dream in the world

green flashes
sparks
cups

LAST NIGHT

Well, rise this time, and leave the body

So it is out into the night tree branches
            Over circle
in the crisp dark night that has no stars.

            And I again enter
            And I go down again

                        to enter swiftly
                        Come down again

Letter to Philip Whalen (1969)

DEAR PHILIP

October 27, 1969. Monday. They are widening the road now, the one in, to 15 feet. It will be refreshing when there are not anymore tractors or trucks grinding the ground into pulp around here. Mr. Calagy Jones had a son at 4:30 this morning. Ebbe is adzing the redwood timbers and Jack is notching them. Larry Kearney read yesterday afternoon at 2. I arranged the timbers into steps for a theater in the bottom of the house. Jack Thibeau, 2 Brazilian poets with unbeatable names, Lewis Warsh, Ebbe, Tom Clark, Richard Duerden, Rod Kennedy, John Thorpe, and assorted pieces of family, four dogs. Mr. Thibeau read when Mr. Kearney gave out. Everyone was hot for more but there wasn't any more. Mr. Duerden was refreshing. He poured some ale I mean wine into his beer, I mean ale can. Mr. Kearney's son had to be boxed on the ear.

Lewis Warsh arrived Sunday. It's about time Don Allen did a book of yours, when you've already become rich and famous, and your popularity poll is up. I saw *On Bear's Head* in paper, on the City Lights counter, last Friday. Along with Richard's new hardbound collection, Creeley's PIECES, *Soul on Ice*, Gurdjieff's *Meeting with Remarkable Men*. Tom Clark felt bad because his book wasn't there. Tom had decided to go in that day with Lewis, and Ebbe went in to the dentist, Jack to the hardware. I bought a Sony taperecorder at KQED. Lewis and Tom went to the *Rolling Stone* office, where Tom accepted the editorship for Poetry and I hope it does him a lot of good, brother. As for myself, I am content to be empress of the world. Then we got on the Kearny street bus, and Lewis and Tom bought boots on Grant Avenue at a place called Highway Robbery. After those were on their feet we walked to Malvina's and met Jack. Lewis picked up his suitcase from Clark Coolidge's and we went to Liam O'Gallaghers, where one of my wooden clogs fell off and made a terrible clatter on my way to a Nepal Tanka. Jack and I went to dinner at Andrew Hoyem's at his press where he lives. We had gin cocktails, and went upstairs to the press, where a candle lighted table was set against the far window, with a stunning view of the old PG&E façade across the street. Lewis and Tom joined us there at nine, for wine and cheese, they had eaten at the Orange Julius on Grant Avenue in China Town. Then Jack drank the sweet vermouth and we turned on the taperecorder. It was a lovely time that we somehow got through. *On Bear's Head* looks much nicer in paper than bound. The cover is nice and chinny, \$3.95. I think everybody will buy a copy, because it's such a bargain now, I'm going into that world and sink myself there for a week, says John Thorpe. I don't know if he was being specific about a week. I think Bill is back with Zoe, but I don't go over for a while. Bill is going to make a movie to go with the tape he and John Thorpe made in various bars. I am going to make a tape of all the songs I can remember, plus a novel. Lewis Warsh looks fine, heavier, so well put together, he must be in his middle twenties now, much more assurance in his intelligence. I hope he likes Bolinas, he is hoping to stay for a while, finding a place, etc. I guess I'm ten years older than he is. I had a lovely surprise visit, one damp cloudy afternoon, from Tom and Aram Saroyan and his wife Gailyn. I had taken some acid, I'm not sure how shell struck I seemed, but he is very high anyway. One mind, one idea. Bell. The wood is started on the house, floor joists. And here comes the caterpillar tractor before my eyes! down the hill!! Take good care of yourself, and hurry up and go around the world so you can come back here. Much lobe, rub,

Joanne

ENSUING PAGES: From *Desecheo Notebook*, designed and printed by Wesley Tanner, Arif Press, 1971.

Joanne Kyger
Desecheo Notebook
150

Saturday

OH fish of the sea
die happily

OH the sea comes in like the mighty
bread and fish

Besides Tom and Peter, Sam Burr
is left on this island. The others
left Thursday when Tom came back
from St. Kitts. Someone stole the
head of N - X. The hermit crabs having
cleaned her bones. An open address
by Peter. Who has stolen her head,
I'm going to search their luggage.
To be left in her natural place.

She rose up in the white raiment
the feminine spirit escaped
as the body began to lose
its life.

Sometime ago caught
rammed through with a spear
and still lays dying
in a black plastic bucket
flopping over
the sign
I sing
OM Sri Maitreya
what for the soul
of a dying fish
stick a knife in its brain
now it is meat, fish meat

Sunday

I know I do not suffer more than anyone
in the whole world
But this morning I had to have first thing
2 cigarettes, half a joint,
a poached egg and corned beef hash, 1 piece toast,
2 cups tea
Jung, Williams, shells, stones,
2 slugs rum, depression, rest of joint,
cigarette, 7 Up, and it's only 10 o'clock
Because I wanted to write a poem
Because I want something to come out of me
You can't try. I believe in life, I am living
now and for a moment the landscape
becomes clear.

A home, a house. I talked with Jack Kerouac
last night. We were sitting under
a rack of clothes, as if it were a clothes
closet. There goes Keith Lampe in a white coat
with blue braid. He's something, isn't he
We agree, we are discussing.

Now there are three large wire enclosures, one with
a wire roof, like they had been tennis courts.
A group of uninformed nature people,
have decided to dump the whole zoo
into these courts, getting the
birds into the one with a top. But OH!
they are inept. The animals can't live together

peacefully. All the jaguars, leopards & ocelots
take out after a rabbit. How did I ever
condone the action of these people. Such naivete!

The more I slow down the harder it is
to all of a sudden move again.
Smaller & smaller until the
speck in side dwindles so small

Generosity: I allow
your existence
equal weight with mine

★

I kick the rock
Rock spirit come out
damn it

★

slowly a string
of beautiful figures drift
from the cave
high up on the rocks
riding through the mists
their diaphanous clothes
flutter
in the grey breeze

★

There was a time
when I wanted
to learn the knowledge
out there
possessed by the world

★

it helps on this island
to do exercise
thoughts stay
in the mind close
to the home camp

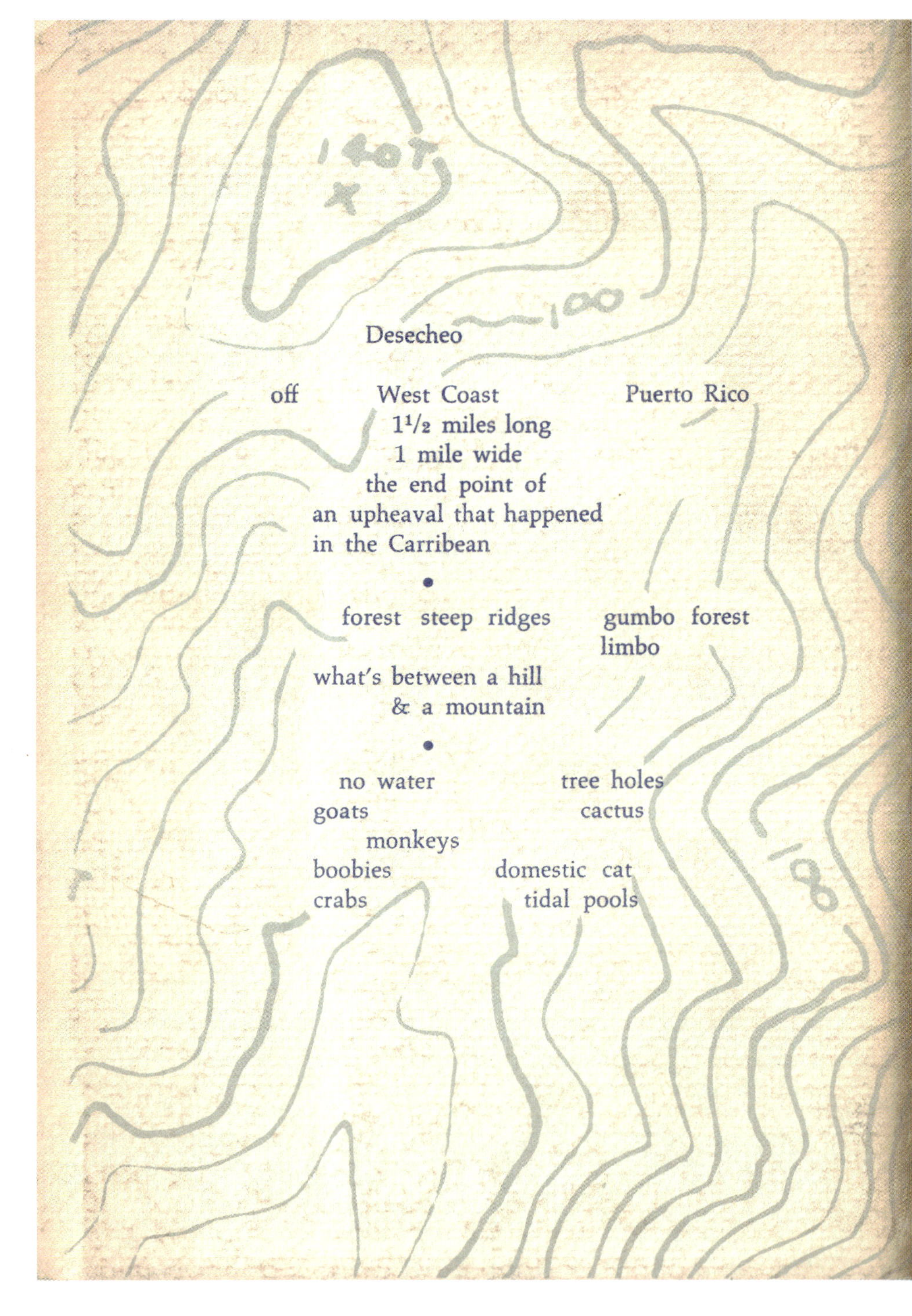

Desecheo

off West Coast Puerto Rico
1½ miles long
1 mile wide
the end point of
an upheaval that happened
in the Carribean

•

forest steep ridges gumbo forest
limbo
what's between a hill
& a mountain

•

no water tree holes
goats cactus
monkeys
boobies domestic cat
crabs tidal pools

Interview with Lawrence Nahem, *Occident*

Lawrence Nahem: You've been a part of the San Francisco literary scene for quite a while. How have you seen that change over the years?

Joanne Kyger: Well it's changed in that the people I originally met in 1958, like, some of them are still around me, like Ebbe Borregaard lives out here. But the people that have remained in this area moved out of San Francisco, like David Meltzer lives over in the Richmond area. Yes, I don't even know what's happening in the San Francisco poetry scene now, or even if there is one.

Have you felt that you've been part of an artistic community?

In some nebulous way, yes. [Laughter.]

I was thinking of the Bolinas group. Seems like a lot of people have come here from New York—

But the living in Bolinas takes over the primary concern I think, because you can't just live here for poetry's sake. I mean that does keep you alive in some really strong way, but the whole practical matter of how you live, what you do with your time, where you get your food from, how you pay your rent—

There's no tightly knit group?

Say, there're poets here and they know each other and they recognize each other as poets and occasionally, you know, one or more—one or more! [Laughter.] One or more will get it on, like Tom Clark and Lewis MacAdams gave a reading at State and they had worked on a collaboration for it.

But it's not anything like a "school"?

Well two years ago we met for a while on Wednesdays and everybody brought their poems and read them, but that was always a little self-conscious. I remember the time that William Everson came and he just wiped out everybody.

How'd that happen?

Well it was incredible. It was when I was living downtown. It was a big room, it was a rainy day, I remember. And everybody was into some kind of land spirit of living here. And he had just such an incredibly painful vision of breaking Christianity on his back and wanting to see the Indians, that it just wiped everybody out. It was just such a heavy spiritual struggle for him, that it was out too far, too far away. He was in his sixties and had just gotten married for the first time.

What's the land spirit, could you elucidate on that?

Oh you just find what a place feels like. Pretty much independent of its people, although the people can reflect it and show you its ways. But it's obvious, the ocean is here, the mountains are here and the weather is always here. And the sun comes up [Laughter], goes down and the stars come out at night. And the feeling in response to those elements.

What influences have helped you in your poetry and who do you listen to now, what do you think's happening now?

Well, early in poetry Robert Duncan and Jack Spicer were my teachers, and then Philip Whalen was a teacher, and Gary Snyder in some very strong respects, and then after that I got pretty much on my own for some years and then when I went to New York I met Lewis Warsh and Anne Waldman and Ted Berrigan and started to get some general drift in that direction; and out here Bill Berkson and Bob Creeley and Tom Clark. As a matter of fact all the poets here now I feel very responsive to, in some way or other. There's Ebbe Borregaard and John Thorpe who used to be here, and Duncan McNaughton and Lewis MacAdams and Larry Kearney and Aram Saroyan—his wife just had a baby yesterday I think, at home by herself, just she and Aram, no doctor.
[The conversation shifts to Ebbe Borregaard.]

Oh, Ebbe's wonderful. He's working on this boat now, he's been working on this boat for ten years. It was built in Egypt and he's rebuilding it and now he's sewing the sails and then he's going to take his great trip out into the ocean, the Unknown . . . *maybe* sometime. [Laughter.] Don't go Ebbe, don't go! It's dangerous out there!

He's going to challenge the elements! [Laughter.]

Ah I don't know, he's got such a great romantic head. He's also a great Blake devotee. And also got further into music than anybody else here, into writing songs and singing them, performing them with a guy named Steve Swallow, a bass player.

Have you ever gotten into other media?

Well I was in television for a year, an experimental television program. And that was exciting, seeing that television could bring all these elements together. I wrote that Descartes piece in *Places to Go* for television. It was put into six sections and each section was acted out with all this fancy video treatment. You could see five or six eyes, or persons, simultaneously.

That's a very strong direction poetry can go in, combining it with other media to make it more powerful. I think there may be certain dangers with it. For example, the ideas we were talking about earlier in regard to John Wieners—that he's doing a very visual performance but does that distract from the content of the poetry?

Well the content is connected with all the other aspects. I know there was a feeling that poetry was needing a helping hand, especially when music was up.

You mean rock and roll?

Yeah. But I think poetry is strong enough. I don't think some poets are *adventuresome* enough about the space they can make. It's very tidy to stay in magazines and books the rest of your life.

So you'd say yes to combining the mediums.

But poetry is those mediums too—poetry is storytelling and it's acting and it is music too and it's theatre.

There's no definition of it before it happens.

Right. Poetry's gotten stuck on the page for an awfully long time, since whenever they invented printing.

Good old Gutenberg. [Laughter] This may be a very hard one. Would you care to describe your lifestyle?

Lifestyle. About getting up in the morning? [Laughter.] Get up in the morning and you look at the day. I had a friend when I first came back to California, about '67, '68, who lived in Mill Valley, who had gotten into acid early. My feeling of him is kind of a guru. And he told me, he said first thing in the morning you get up and you get *stoned*, and he said, I don't mean just a little stoned, get *really stoned*.

So I tried that for a while and it really did start to change my life, because of all those habit patterns I'd been used to . . . So then I put some coffee on and go stand outside a little bit, and maybe I'll think about doing some meditation—I'll *think* about it. [Laughter.]

That's where it is in the nineteen seventies.

Then if it's a good day I'll putter around the garden and then have some breakfast and then go get the mail and go downtown to see what's happening—

[Tongue in cheek.] What do you mean by puttering around the garden?

Puttering around? You go over and pull something up, pick something up and— [Laughter.]

Put it back.

Put a shovel in it. Oh you pull weeds and mulch a little, just check it out, see what's going on, new spiders around, and what's coming up. Then either walk or drive downtown. And during this time there's all the things you think about that you're going to do or that you have to do, and then you have to give up on those immediately—you can't think about what you're going to do and what you have to do. [Laughter.] And you go down to the store, you kind of stand in the middle of the store for a while and then it'll start to drift back to you why you're in a store. And then I'll often go sit down by the ocean on the good days and I'll go back up and maybe stop off and see the Creeleys or . . . visit around.

It's about 3:30 now?

About 1 or 2. That could be the settling down period for a good hour or two long conversation with someone, which people can come in or out of. Then you pull yourself together with a start and say, I have some things to do! [Laughter.] So, checking over the things to do, you do one or two of them. [Laughter.] Cook dinner and maybe in the evening go to Smiley's.

Smiley's is the bar?

Yeah, that's like the only open community place in Bolinas, other than going and visiting people—it's a wonderful place to go. I look at downtown Bolinas sometimes as a big stage set, in which just to watch what the action is about is fascinating.

Do you write very often?

Well, I keep a notebook. I've kept them for a long time. And that just gets to nothing more than sometimes writing down the date. See, this is not a very interesting notebook, I've been struggling with it . . . I get things in here like, 'The gift of a mystery is often the removal of a taboo." Little aphoristic statements. Also I like notebooks just for the mundane stuff you can put down, like addresses and telephone numbers and also lists that you can make for yourself—the endless list, the universal list, the eternal list! [Laughter.] Trying to organize your head into the objects of attention, to remind you that those are going to cause or not cause action later on. And notebooks are good because they *are* books and when you've finished writing one you've written a book, it's already bound up. It's the only copy of it.

What happens to them?

Just put them on a shelf . . . It's a little history of whatever you choose to write down, whatever you chose to put in, paste up.

Do you use that material, work it into the poems?

Yeah, I've gone through and I'll pull stuff out, and often it goes into a poem. Then when you get down to the typewriter that's a lot easier because it comes out in a more clearly printed form.

How do you feel strong relationships affect your writing?

Well strong relationships are a sustenance of poetry, because any strength of emotion that you have takes itself into the content of what you're writing, and the stronger the better. Because everybody knows the isolated, "who's out there?" feeling; you know, when you have this individual poetry that wants to move out. In an ideal way I believe in a group poetry, a group of people writing in and out of the same situation, because that's the only way a voice gets strong.

But some writers, for example James Joyce, seem to gain their strength by being alone, through their isolation.

Okay, say, that's how you get a lot of writing done. But I think the less that's held private for that strength the better, although it's risky, because you can lose it.

That's a danger that I see, that in a group you just get your voice meshed in, you wouldn't be able to distinguish it—

But that's great. See that's the idea about losing what you think is individual. I don't see how you get strong unless you do that, unless everybody goes in and out of each other's stories or words or sounds or plots or themes. Say, look at poets like Allen, Gary, Philip Whalen, and Lew, who have some kind of vision and understanding in common, in which their voices are connected in some way. I mean, it could be all the components of one story, and they all revolve in it.

Yeah, it's like a vortex. They're reflecting on each other. I think it's true that, at the least, the friendship strengthens your nerve, your sense that you're doing something important.

That's like when Tom Clark and Lewis MacAdams were doing their reading together, they were at beautiful space places mixing up Shakespeare and baby talk—but they did point out what they had in common was a lot of nerve. [Laughter.] And I thought, wow, that's it! I felt so refreshed by it.

How do you see yourself in the role of poet?

Well, when you get into poetry you connect yourself to the ages of poetry, whatever your imagination of it is or whatever you know about it, however long it's gone back, however you can relate to it. For a while I was really high on the historic Poet, because I knew the names of these poets, as far back—let's see, Greece was as far back as I got for a while.

Those myths enter much of your work, as in Tapestry and the Web.

Tapestry and the Web. That was the first time I met a story that I could be inside, and it invited me. That's when I was 22, 23. And I could fall in and out of that story for some time. And that's how I learned that there was a big Story that was going on. I spent a lot of time thinking about the big Story that's going on! [Laughter.]

Capital "s"?

Yeah. And feeling like I'm in parts of it at times.

It's an occupation for an artist to keep sensitized, to keep the nerves open, an occupational hazard so to speak. Lew Welch says he cracked up behind the weirdness of being a poet. Have you gotten close to that, does being a poet ever throw you onto the edge?

Well . . . I don't mind those edges. [Laughter.] Sometimes it's too exacting for me. I'd love to give up poetry. And then a couple times I thought, oh I'm sick and tired of it, it's too hard, I don't want to have to answer magazines, I don't want to have to push myself out there—

Exposure can be a painful thing.

Well it gets to be less, it's not painful in that respect. I mean it's not private anymore if you choose to show it. But then poetry can be boring for someone else to read, because everybody knows pain and everybody's tired to death of it. And that's a big drag. So, the only thing that comes to me is that I don't push ahead enough or do enough or put it out there more, you know, it's like I can just sit and it can come to me, and then, "Where am I supposed to take it?" is a real question for me sometimes; and that's not just for my individual self, it's like living here for example, how do we give the town poetry? Where do you give poetry, where does it go? The magazine scene is just—anybody can do that at this point. So I get hung up on what is the real force of poetry, how can it be stronger, how can it get really strong, how can it get stronger in myself. And how to keep the word from faltering, or how do you find the great Hero, how do you bring the new Hero in, how do you keep the vision open.

It seems to me that that involves two things: keeping your own channels open, and attempting to get it out there.

And trying to figure out what out there is all about, too.

What's your thought on that? How do you feel about poetry readings, to be specific?

I dig poetry readings, a lot. They're something I always feel that I'm not quite prepared for, but I realize it's a really necessary thing for a poet to do, to bring his own voice to something, and that it's always a fantastic testing ground. There's always the dreams before the performance!

What rewards do you find in being a poet, what advantages are there?

Well once you're into poetry and it gets into your life you can't turn back from it. Oh you could become complacent I suppose and then always keep writing the same kind of poems, but for me it gets into . . . I was going to say, adventure of the self, but maybe that's too particular. For me it's always a process of just trying to keep pushing out the horizon . . . The advantage of being a poet? The advantage of being a poet is you get to know other poets! [Laughter.]

That's like Duchamp saying he was much more interested in artists than in art; he didn't want to go to the museums anymore but he loved getting to know the painters. [Laughter.] So poetry becomes part of your life and obviously there are no tangible rewards; it's just part of the adventure of the self.

Well poetry itself is the reward. It's like, how it turns you on and turns you off.

Can you see poetry as having a particular function for you, any personal function?

Keeping your hand in. Keep your hand in, keep your ear in, keep your voice in. You can think of it as a meditation, it's a location that you start to find the more you go into it, so it's a place that's there and the longer you're away from it the harder it is to get back to it. Or sometimes it's not. But it's a real place, whatever writing space you go to.

Have you been away from it for long periods of time?

It always seems long when you're away from it. Oh yeah I've gone through all different changes. My feeling about what the poem is has changed a lot. I write things down—say, keeping a notebook you can write anything down, one word even—and then there's the decision as to why is that in poetry. Is poetry something you should be concerned about as an abstraction? If you're inside it, it even feels like an awkward word to say.

Dylan said he'd rather be called a trapeze artist than a poet.

I think it took me till I was about thirty—no, it must have been longer than that—before that became an identity that I was within; and before that it was my own longings or definitions of it, but I think it takes—it does take—when other people start to see it. I mean, poetry can pass for me really fast. And so I don't really think about myself in relationship, say, to that book [*Places to Go*]. I almost feel that somebody else wrote it. So with that behind you, it's something outside yourself that's been created, that sits there. And so when that starts to build up, say, let's say, books or things like that . . .

Can you define how your sense of the poem has changed?

I used to think of it as having more of a form. Like you sit down and write a poem—but this isn't poetry this is prose, or this is not a poem, why isn't this a poem. And now I think almost anything that a poet wants to call a poem is a poem. Like Aram Saroyan's "eyeye."

The other night I told that to a friend; that, for example, there's Aram Saroyan who's doing "eyeye," and she said, "That's a poem?" [Laughter.] And I said, "That's a poem." I mean, how can you define it, why not?

Space starts to get really compacted. Also I've moved a lot from linear space—and I've learned a lot from Tom Clark and, I suppose, different drugs—that linear space was not a space that I really thought or experienced in. Although it's a good space for your head to follow at times—drop a little linear space in just to reassure people! [Laughter.] But that space is really, like, *chunks* of things, and that a word reverberates . . . that's why one word can be a poem. As long as it'll reverberate and keep doing that vibration of meaning, then it works. I really like phrases now that have some internal turning, that seem to turn around all the time inside. So it even gets out of meaning after a while, it gets into being a mantra or it just hangs in a different way in the air.

I often get that from your poetry, that the line isn't just a concrete thing, it keeps going, the attention is constantly moving forward fast.

That's Olson too: one perception directly follows upon the tail of the next. It always interests me to see how the mind connects something; say, in this conversation we're more or less keeping in a connective space. It's not—say, it was called free association—but just say the mind connects one thing after another. And it seems to do it, it doesn't demand that it have all the little explanations filled in between.

That gets to the question of what kind of coherence you're looking for. What kinds of things re-occur in your work?

Occur? The weather. I you me. Peter. Change. Shifting. I'm really landed right now. When I wrote *Desecheo Notebook* I was in another physical location that allowed other things to go on . . . I feel sometimes I'm just in a lot of mind-tripping and reviewing, so that I can get out to a place where it finally will sit for a while, outside of time, of the usual time. I remember once I had an experience with John Thorpe. We were downtown and I don't know how we got into it but we got into this space where finally everything was in the other time. I don't know if you've been really high sometimes—?

Yeah.

When everything starts to look solid, outside of usual time. I thought it was mythic; finally the story was apparent, what was going on, which is what goes on anyway, but finally another kind of chatter had ceased. And it's that kind of place that I try to get to a lot.

I find in much of your poetry an attempt to define the self, even to correct it. "I have reminded myself not to frown or grimace as these are unpleasant faces . . ." Also the Descartes piece, with, for example, its "PROVISORY CODE OF MORALS."

You mean self-examination? Well yeah, but that can also be a hangup too. I think you have to get beyond self-examination. And in fact you could say that there is no self . . . *no self.*

I've got it right here. "Well I myself am not myself," from a poem of yours in Big Sky *[magazine].*

That's right.

But then you are actually trying to talk to yourself in the poetry to change yourself.

You talk to yourself in order to hear yourself talk, or to hear your typewriter talk or something like that. I mean who are you really talking to? You're just a voice, a voice out there talking to itself about itself, going through its changes, gymnastics, watch-my-mind gymnastics. I think that can get to be a terrible preoccupation.

Do you feel that the process of writing involves "inspiration"? Jack Spicer uses the term "dictated writing," for example.

Well, a lot of it I see is the strength of what words are, I mean, they're ancient before us. And we're using English, and you go into those words and they definitely have their own strength and the place they want to go. And it's like you're new in it, one is new in the time, but you're not really because it's inherited. And yeah, words come through you, one doesn't invent them. You can bully them around so much, but then after a while they'll really just refuse to work at all. And how you can get yourself loose enough so that you allow to come out what wants to come out, without trying to dictate it or formalize it or make sense of it—and the less you try to make sense out of what comes out of you the better it is! Because those periods and thoughts can be coercive, at times, to some deeper flow.

1974

Robert Creeley

I really got to know Robert Creeley, as a neighbor, when he moved to Bolinas in 1970. Lots of time was spent around his table with his wife Bobbie—multiple conversations going on with the poets who dropped in to have a glass of the ubiquitous Almaden white wine. Then he took off for a reading trip through the Pacific, Hong Kong, Australia, New Zealand on February 29, 1976, during which time he wrote his book *HELLO*, and that was the end of his Bolinas residence.

Bolinas when he lived here in the early '70s had many young poets with their new families trying to figure out how to live in the "country." Tom Clark, poetry editor of the *Paris Review*, was one of the first to move out onto the mesa with his wife, Angelica. They bought a house and had a daughter. Other poet friends followed, many from the East Coast. "New York Refugees Go Home" was painted on the seawall at the downtown beach. Tom said to me once, and it has resonated ever since, it's not what you Say as a poet, it's how you Live as a poet. And that is what Bob, with a great deal of clarity, comfort, simplicity, and style knew how to do. He was organized—and in the somewhat inventive hippie environment of the time—a great model. He demonstrated a new carpet sweeper to me with a great deal of pride. I didn't even know they made them anymore. It was a sleek, efficient model. Of course I had no carpets at the time, but it was an iconic symbol of Keeping the House Clean!

Plus, he was the only poet I knew that actually earned his living for himself and his family as a poet and a teacher. And he had the big important East Coast publisher—Scribner's.

His long poem "PEOPLE" preceded his move here. His old friend from Mallorca days, artist Arthur Okamura, had done a series of drawings made up of tiny tiny people, who made all sorts of shapes—flowers, spirals, starbursts. Shambhala Press was to publish the book with just the drawings, but Arthur felt another element was needed and sent the drawings to Creeley to see if he wanted to write some words. It was a happy collaboration, and the book has a spacious, joyously affirmative quality. It was redolent of the magic and longings of the time—the flower people, the little people, the spirit people. "I knew where they were, in the woods. My sister made them little houses . . . They live now in everything . . . not isolated but meld into continuous place, one to one, never alone . . . I want to go home."

And Bolinas was his home for many years until a new direction and family opened out to him.

> Bolinas and me. Believe me . . . Let's walk down to the beach, see the sea, say. I want to walk around here, look at the people, pretty, look at the houses, stop in the bar, get the mail, get going again somewhere . . . Things move. You've come to here, and are here.
>
> (from BOLINAS AND ME: A DAY BOOK)

There were no limits on being "here" in the moment. Excursions and almost childlike gleeful adventures: "I must have been around water last night because my clothes are all wet."

What wonder more
Than to be
Where you are
And to know it

We're walking together on the beach and he points up to the clouds in the sky, "Can you see the castles up there?" Castles? It never occurred to me. He starts to look like King Arthur. He talks about the "kingdom."

He says, "Poetry occupies a moment of time. If I manage to gain the articulation necessary *in* that moment, then happily there is a poem."

And one can add, poetry happens in a place—an intimate place of people with attendant cause and effect. Bill Berkson's record player has to be taken often to the record player doctor after late nights when Bob stops by, after the bar has closed, with pal, writer Bill Brown, to play Eric Dolphy exuberantly. So that the expensive little tone arm is broken while Bill is asleep. But the jazz must continue.

Bob gives me a copy of just published A DAY BOOK. NOVEMBER 19—on my birthday, which is November 19, inscribed "for Joanne on her birthday." I thought, how nice, everything goes together.

One day after another
Perfect
They all fit.

Interview with Stephanie Anderson, *The Conversant*

COVER ILLUSTRATIONS BY PHILIP WHALEN, DONALD GURAVICH, AND ARTHUR OKAMURA

This is a series of ongoing interviews with women actively engaged with small-press publishing between the 1950s and 1980s. It comes from a desire not only to preserve their accounts but also to draw wider attention to the vital role of women editors and publishers in the mimeograph revolution and beyond. In these decades "poems were bouncing off the sidewalk" (Maureen Owen), and this series traces some of those madcap trajectories. This conversation was conducted from December 2013 to May 2014 via email, while Joanne Kyger was in Oaxaca and away from the Hearsay *archives.*

Stephanie Anderson: How did the Bolinas Hearsay News *begin? Were you involved in its founding?*

Joanne Kyger: Before the *Bolinas Hearsay News* started publication in 1974, there were three small irregularly published papers, *The Bolinas Hit*—Bill Beckman publisher—*Beaulines*, and *The Paper*.

I remember the first copies of the *Hearsay* being written on paper plates down at Scowley's, one of the two local eateries. Greg Hewlett had organized fund-raisers earlier to buy the town a press. Through spaghetti dinners and donations, a multilith was purchased and housed in a garage on the mesa. It was later moved to Mickey Cummings' house a few blocks away and he was the first official printer of the "Mesa Press." Bill Berkson published some of his early Big Sky books on it. While still housed there, the first *Hearsay*s came out. They would often be collated downtown at Scowley's, and then distributed locally, as they are now, at three or four downtown businesses, and in a mailbox outside the *Hearsay* office.

The *Hearsay* was offered a space in the building behind the Bolinas Public Utilities Office in the middle '70s and remains there to this day.

I helped the Wednesday editor, Nancy Whitefield, with the paper for several years before it moved to the BCPUD office, when it was at Bill Johnson's house. He was a talented and playful graphic artist and the mornings were long with coffee, brandy, and long pauses for inspiration when no articles were handed in. But the paper was always delivered to the printer by noon. A calendar of events is still the main front-page feature, with birthdays listed in another column. It was a way for the town to find out what was going on, and remains a mainstay of information about musical events, happenings at the Community Center, meetings, etc.

I became the Wednesday editor on my own in 1984, and usually asked someone to be an "assistant" editor in order to bring other elements of news and events into the paper. Bolinas is an unincorporated

THE WEDNESDAY
HEARSAY NEWS

OCTOBER 4 , 2000 33¢

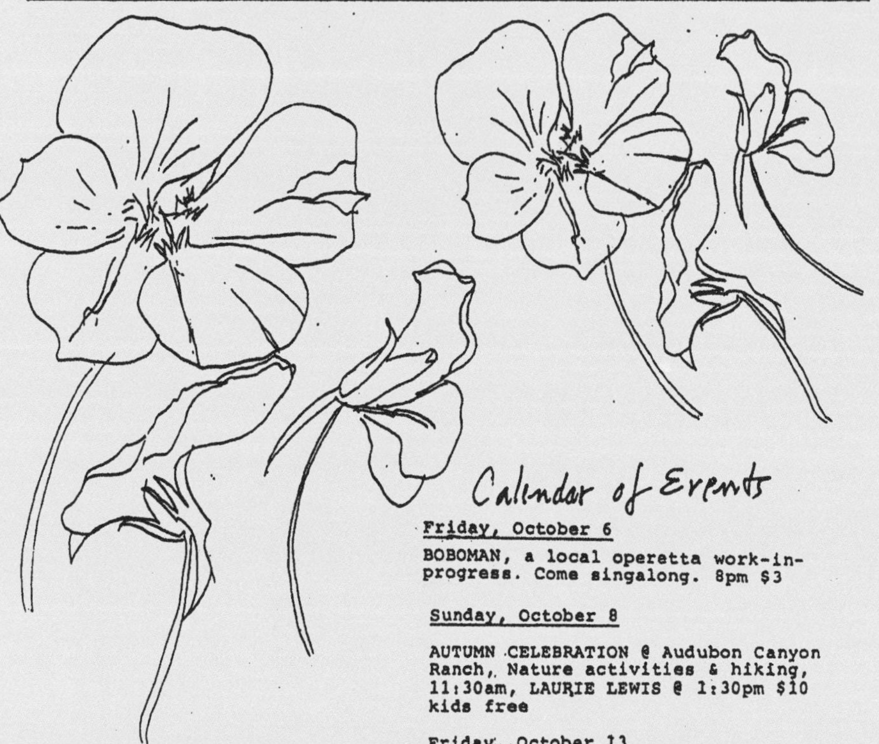

Calendar of Events

Friday, October 6

BOBOMAN, a local operetta work-in-progress. Come singalong. 8pm $3

Sunday, October 8

AUTUMN CELEBRATION @ Audubon Canyon Ranch, Nature activities & hiking, 11:30am, LAURIE LEWIS @ 1:30pm $10 kids free

Friday, October 13

CELTIC MUSIC w Athena Tergis, Laura Risk & Steve Boughman, @ Community Center, 8pm

Haiku for Mike

Bouquet of HUGE
nasturtium leaves
"HOW can I support myself?"

Philip Whalen

Today's Editor Joanne Kyger
Press True Heitz
Cover Drawing Philip Whalen

town, but we have three elected bodies that represent us to the county: the Bolinas-Stinson School, the Fire Department, and the Bolinas Public Utilities District—the latter acts as a public forum for any issues that concern the town, which are brought up at the beginning of its monthly meetings. The *Hearsay* published all the minutes for these meetings, plus those of the Bolinas Community Center, which owns the main building downtown where different town events take place.

All articles accepted by the *Hearsay*, which are dropped off during the mornings when the paper is laid out or dropped in the mail slot in the door, must be signed. I think that is the only editorial requirement.

Could you say more about the genre of the Hearsay News? *It seems a bit like a free-for-all, in terms of content. What distinguished it from the three small papers published before it?*

The fact that it was reliably published three times a week and had a calendar of events.

Sometimes it's difficult—or impossible—to find a "masthead," then or now, for the Hearsay News. *Was anonymity something prized, or did the community simply know everyone involved in production?*

Mastheads were various; editors could use whatever they wanted, as long as they remembered to notate the date and day of the week.

One thing that strikes me in the first issues of the Hearsay *from 1974 is the little pieces of art and poetry (including a* Hearsay *limerick contest!) tucked away among the lost and found notices, etc. Were those items filler, or were they meant to have the same import as more "practical" news? Did the* Hearsay News *ever publish items by those visiting (or residing) poets and artists?*

The *Hearsay* editors could publish anything they wanted to fill up the paper. I always liked using poems from visiting poets. The graphics often came from visitors also. When I was editor I relied on Donald Guravich frequently for drawings and covers. The copy machine we used as a vital part of our layout design could reduce or enlarge drawings. Local pieces from contributors came first before reprints of other articles, even though they were about Bolinas. All this was laid out during morning office hours 9–12, and then the printer came in and ran off the copies and took them downtown by at least 3 or 4 that afternoon.

When you say, "Local pieces from contributors came first before reprints of other articles, even though they were about Bolinas," does that mean that work by residents always came first, regardless of content? What kind of reprints would you consider?

Articles about Bolinas printed in the *San Francisco Chronicle*, magazines, other newspapers, etc. There were always lots of pieces about Bolinas tearing down the road sign on Highway One that said with an arrow BOLINAS 2. Like it was a town that never wanted to be found by the casual driver, tourist. They made local bumper stickers that said BOLINAS 2 and people would drive all over California with them. It actually was a mysterious advertisement.

How many copies were printed?

When I first moved here in 1969 there were about 500 people who lived here full time. Now there are about 1,500. People share copies of the paper, and there is always a copy at the downtown library. There are anywhere from 100–250 copies printed, depending on whether there are big election issues in which everyone wants a voice. Now that it is online I'm not sure how many copies are printed. I stopped being the Wednesday editor about a year ago.

In the age of instant information and global news, what are some of the benefits and challenges of the Hearsay's *localism—of publishing for and about such a specific community?*

It certainly keeps a community glued together. Birth announcements, weddings, deaths; announcements concerning roads, water usage, the Fire Department, the school, etc., and agendas for meetings for all pertinent organizations, including the Community Center. Also the minutes taken at these meetings are published. It makes the "government" here much more transparent. The paper works as a community bulletin board in which everyone is a "reporter"—the only requirement being that you sign your name. The display ads and classified ads are local and very useful in moving goods and services around.

The phrase "everyone is a 'reporter'" reminds me of the idea that the typewriter makes it possible for everyone to be a "publisher." What technological changes did you witness at the Hearsay *over your thirty-plus years of editing? And did you publish poems in the* Hearsay*?*

Not everyone had a typewriter or printer. Many pieces were, and still are, written out by hand. We tried to aim for a three-and-a-half-inch column width. So one could be a publisher if you had machine that could make multiple pages. I never published any of my own poems, but Steve Heilig who became an alternate Wednesday editor, published some of my work. I never heard anyone mention what they thought about my writing. I tried to keep a fairly translucent role as editor, publishing whatever was turned in, and with a backup of articles relevant to the community to use as filler when needed. One of the editors, Stuart Chapman made some official-looking laminated *Hearsay News* press passes, which some "reporters" have used to gain access to things like the Democratic Convention here in the '80s, and various theater events.

The Bolinas Hearsay News

OCTOBER 15, 2008 WEDNESDAY 33 CENTS

INSIDE TODAY'S PAPER:
AUGUST 20 BCPUD MINUTES:
Dwaileebe project opposed by people present at meeting...
In a letter in support of Mr. Dwaileebe oppostion is characterized as 'malcontents' and part of group beating near Brighton Beach....

TONIGHT AT 11PM
replay on Channel 9 of
TRULY, CALIFORNIA's
The Bolinas Lagoon

Gold-crown sparrows, finding an air draft, greet their happiness with chirps. They participate in the earth's vigor. By night's fall their energies are dissipated. That's when some people mix wine with beer. They dream of their tribe of origin.

Small towns suit the full moon. In the bars, loud music increases the natural weariness of the customers. The season is undamaged but there's danger in the grass. An apprehension of things to come. That woman doesn't shoot heroin, being naturally high. Fate is cruel and its damage irreparable.

--from SEASONS
by Etel Adnan
The Post Apollo Press 2008

Birthday Greetings

October 13:	Julia Rose Cummings Phil Butler Lynn Copp Stever Auer Roger Sierra
October 14:	Annie Crotts
October 15:	Jerry Bohlman Jason Rodgers Angela Rollins Ruby Lee
October 16:	Kiowa Broek
October 17:	Heather Peacock Kathy Sayers
October 18:	Jane Okamura Sanders Peter Gubbins
October 19:	Magda Micah Ashley Ratcliffe Candra Docherty Stephen Haney Perry Hooper Richard Schoenherz

FULL MOON

The full moon rises on Wednesday, October 15th; this moon is referred to as the Hunter's Moon; an extra bit of light for hunting before winter sets in. It is called the 'fallin leaves time' among the Nez Perce of the northwest. The moon is followed by the Orionid meteor showers (Orion the hunter), formed from the dust of the tail of Haley's Comet. They will be difficult to see this year because of a bright moon rising. Extra high tides are expected as the moon is at perigee--closest to the earth. The highest day will be Wednesday and Thursday with 6.6 tides mid-day.

--Loretta Farley, Park Ranger
from West Marin Citizen 10/9/'08

Today's Wednesday Editor:
Joanne Kyger
Cover Drawing: Donald Guravich

Did working on the Hearsay *change your ideas about publishing and/or how you approach your creative work?*

I found out how easy it was to lay out a page (8½ × 17), what designs and space worked best. Actually I found out how easy it was to publish something once the "right" setup is there, and have it on the street on the same day.

We did a few publications on the press, called it Evergreen Road Press, and published a few issues of a small magazine called *GATE* with Stefan Hyner, who then published it on a bigger scale in Germany, where he lived.

You've published some e-books; do you feel like the immediacy of the internet is similar to the oftlauded immediacy of mimeo publication?

I'm not aware of any e-books I've published. What are they? The internet is quickly accessible, but unless you print out what you're reading, it isn't as easily available for a return read—which one wants to do with magazines and poetry.

I found the e-books on your EPC author page.

Found the two e-books; forgot about them. Coyote Books' *The Distressed Look* was also in a small paper edition form. *Permission by the Horns* was eventually unsatisfactory since it wasn't in a paper form.

What do you think makes poetry or magazines something you want to see in print, to "return read" as you say?

I think poetry is something you need to read more than once—unlike headlines in a newspaper.

What was your favorite aspect of being Wednesday editor?

I liked being able to "produce" a publication/newspaper in one day. Very gratifying to see it all distributed at the various stores downtown and at the library. For some years there was home delivery by a crew of young kids on bikes. And also I liked meeting other members of the community who came to the office with articles or questions or to place a classified ad. One could get a feel for the ephemeral but personal sense of what makes up "the news" in a small community.

Why did you stop being Wednesday editor?

THE WEDNESDAY

HEARSAY NEWS

January 15, 2003 33¢

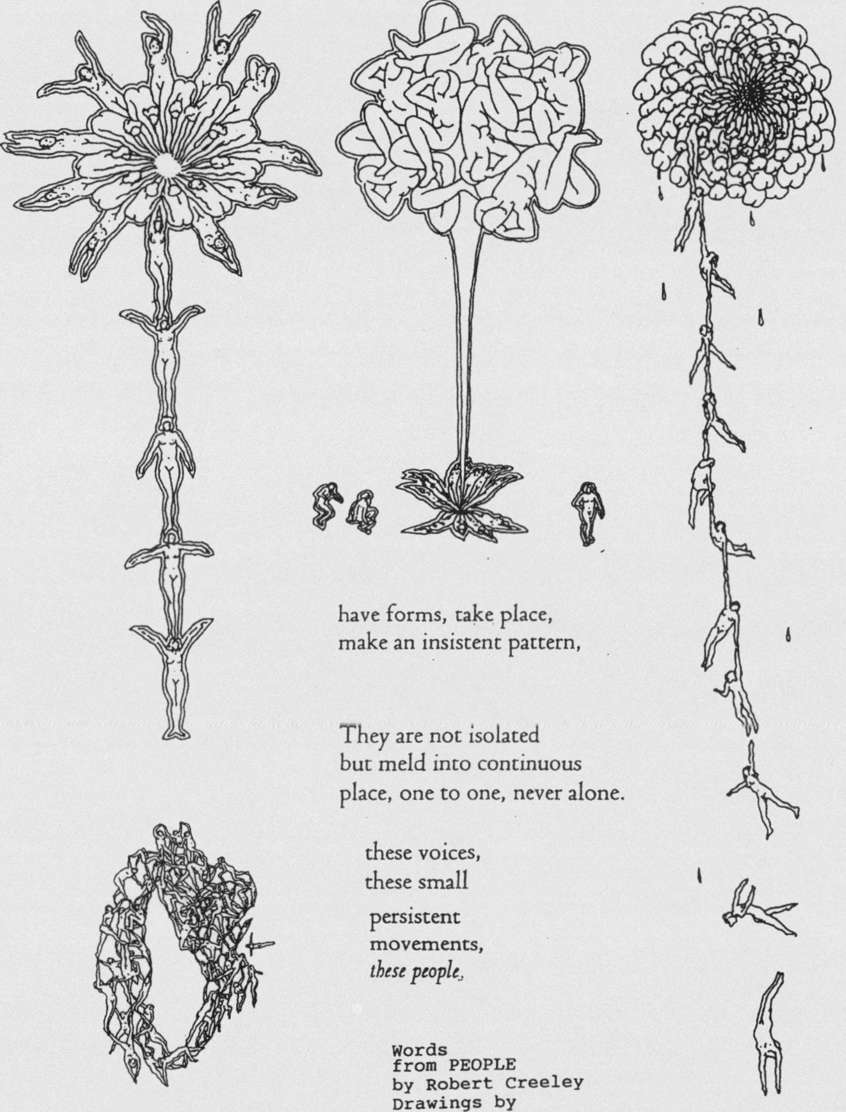

have forms, take place,
make an insistent pattern,

They are not isolated
but meld into continuous
place, one to one, never alone.

these voices,
these small
persistent
movements,
these people,

Saturday January 18
MARCH AGAINST US
INVASION OF IRAQ
in San Francisco
(details inside)

Words
from PEOPLE
by Robert Creeley
Drawings by
Arthur Okamura

Today's editor
Joanne Kyger
Press
True Heitz

I thought I would take a break from the paper for a while, and that while kept getting longer. New editors eventually stepped in, reflecting another side of Bolinas. One has to watch a tendency as editor to write articles advertising oneself.

What's special and/or ordinary about Bolinas, a place that I feel has become almost mythological for poets and artists? You've lived abroad; why Bolinas for the last thirty-plus years?

Bolinas is very beautifully situated in front of the coast range, on a lagoon and a mesa. Surrounded by protected parkland. I bought my house and land here in 1972 when it was still very inexpensive. I found for a while I had to save up to be able to get out of town, which is always useful for perspective. It's very easy to live here, but one needs to make an hour's drive over the coast range to larger towns to do any extensive shopping for groceries, hardware, clothes, etc.

Sounds like a lovely and insular community. Did that make the arrival of visiting poets and artists especially important for the community? (I'm thinking of Joe Brainard's Bolinas Journal *and all the different people he mentions meeting.)*

For the poets, it was always wonderful to have visiting poets. I'm not sure what the rest of the community thought.

Apart from the Hearsay News*, what were the other kinds of publishing ventures with which you were involved (as editor, helper, etc.)? (I'm thinking of* The Turkey Buzzard Review *and* Wild Dog*—would you talk about those? Were there others?)*

The Turkey Buzzard Review was a loose gathering of friends, mostly women, who got together and drank coffee and brandy and decided what to publish. Dottie LeMieux was the most ambitious, so we decided she would be editor. We gave several "theatrical" Turkey Buzzard readings for the community. It was always fun and barely serious. Some years before I helped edit *Wild Dog*, which moved from Idaho to San Francisco in 1965–66, when I was living there.

The 1971 oil spill had a galvanizing effect on the Bolinas community. Do you think that that event influenced the literary/publishing scene? (And if so, how?)

Kevin Opstedal does a good and accurate job of talking about Bolinas "Literary" history in *Dreaming as One* which title he has since changed to *All This Every Day*. It still hasn't been published outside of being online and a few Xerox copies, one of which is at the library. He covers the oil spill accurately, which does give a picture of the "rest" of the community, the non-poet and very active participants. It did start a very active political participation in the town's problems, and subsequent participation on the Bolinas Community Public Utility board, elected offices. Lewis MacAdams' *News from Niman Farm* is a great reflection of that time. He was an elected member of the board, and the only poet.

> *Opstedal calls the* Hearsay News *a "community forum" and an "ongoing biography of the town, a true and immediate diary of community consciousness." Is this an apt description?*

Kevin is right on with his comments about the *Hearsay News*.

2014

I don't want to repeat
the same mistakes over again,
or the mistakes somebody else made just so
I can have the experience of them. See, fucked
up again. Live and learn. And off the excessive
fondness for one's own self knowledge, un-
tested, but reigning supreme. That leads me
more astray, every day. What we commonly
know in the air, in our dreams, what chooses
continually & continually to grow, the obvious
under our noses, is this life. Yearning is blind-
ness. The weed has a name, is quite proud of it-
self, builds a community with other weeds, birds
hop through. The imported domestic is a labor
of love, but a labor, such a labor. At home here,
no single thought is my thought. It whispers
through the air in sweet misty fog,
in bright sky blue.

KENT STATE ARTS FESTIVAL

Kent State Arts Panel

JOANNE KYGER WITH RICHARD BLEVINS, ED DORN, AND JOEL OPPENHEIMER

Richard Blevins: We've discussed the poetic line for three sessions. Could you talk about your sense of the movement of your line?

Joanne Kyger: Well, in my first book [*The Tapestry and the Web*] the line to me was where it was really at. And if you could move the line around, you could really move. And I really felt finally that the line was the extension of my arm. Now, you see, I'm off linear poetry.

What do you mean by linear poetry?

The line. At one point it was very important for me to feel that a line could move and shift exactly. You could move a line around very carefully and that really dictated the movement of how the poem was going to move, how the voice was going to move in a certain way, and how your physical speech moved through the line.

My first book of poetry was set on a linotype machine and I realized there was a vast difference between my typewriter space and where my head space was, and where the printed space was. They didn't print it with any sense of where the line was moving, and it was very clear to me that the line moved in this rhythmic way. It moved back and forth across the page. It wasn't set with any definition about how the line moved. I realized the line moved in juxtaposition to the line above itself, but very exactly. When it was first set the line could be anywhere on the page. So I finally ended up by saying the line moves in relationship to the letter, the word above it.

You determined that by rhythm?

No. The line to me was physical space. It was my attempt to make rhythm, to make the line move in a very exact manner.

I noticed that when you read your voice moves to the end of the line to a rising stop. How does this rising stop relate to the configuration of the line on the page?

FACING: Broadside for Kent State Arts Festival (1974). Woodblock design by Michael Myers, printed by Holbrook Teter, Zephyrus Image Press.

The rising voice. That's just to keep it open.

The line meant to me the physical body. It meant a landscape. You lay out your physical body and your physical body goes thru your hand, and you lay that out on the page. It was like a landscape line. Now, I don't feel that precious or exact about handling the line that way because I'm more into a voice line, and the poem gets to be more like a score, a score for the voice though. And so I'm not trying to make it that exact. Didn't Williams say that: if you get it exactly on the page any voice can play it. And then I realized I was getting finicky. It has to do with printers.

RB: At the reading you broke off into singing.

I would like to sing more. I heard Allen Ginsberg last week outside San Francisco and I realized his poems are into chanting and singing. So it's a natural extension of where the voice wants to go.

Ed Dorn: I can follow this talk about the line, and can hear what you're saying. Linear poetry is like a conservative line. I never heard it put that way. It sounds right.

RB: When you said linear poetry I thought you meant a poem that moves in a straight line directly from the top of the page to the bottom of the page.

When I did the last part of my first book, "The Odyssey Poems," I really diagrammed them. Yes, there is a straight line, like diagramming an English sentence. I put a straight line down the middle and made everything branch off like a tree. It had its roots on the ground and then things branch off from either side of it. You could fit all the voices and patterns that got into the movement that way.

Joel Oppenheimer: I assumed that what you meant when you said you were not interested in the linear poems was that you meant you were no longer going to worry about where any individual line ended. What you were concerned with was the whole trip thru the poem.

Oh, I really think about the individual line. I think every line ought to be able to stand by itself.

JO: Well, I'm lost.

By linear I mean a mode or manner of speaking in which you go thru a linear progression and you end up with a conclusion.

JO: Ah, it's linear thinking then.

Linear thinking that goes with the linear line. So at this point the kind of space that interests me is the kind of space that vibrates its meaning. It's the one-liner or the sampler on the wall. It just stays there for a long time. You can go back into that one line and it will keep giving off overtones. It's connected but it's a different kind of space.

Student: Could you connect that with music in some way?

Well, how I make that work now—and I'm not really clear on that solution—is that I carry the beat inside me and that connects up with the phrases. So rhythmically that's shown in the couple of pieces I've done in which they are just phrases, and what happens to me when I do this is that, ah, when I get a beat and then I can just put those phrases inside that beat, with some pauses and rests between them. There's no way really to show that on the page clearly except that I assume that when it builds up its own rhythm after a while you can read it.

Student: Do you have difficulty transcribing your voice?

Once you get the line down I think you can be a little freer about how you can put it down. The notation system. Trust the words; words have their own strength, so it's not a matter of personality to carry.

Student: Some of your words look like they're organized in paragraphs.

Yes, I'm into the paragraph a lot now, because it gives me a sense of continuity. Yes, I guess I get tired of the lines. A paragraph is a big breath, if you blow it, so once you get into it, it automatically sets up its own rhythm and boundaries.

1974

FOLLOWING PAGES: From *Trip Out and Fall Back*, designed and printed by Wesley Tanner, Arif Press, 1974. Covers by Gordon Baldwin.

JK
TRIP OUT & FALL BACK
Joanne Elizabeth Kyger

Peter Rowan and I are walking down Mesa Road.
He asks me who are my teachers. I don't want
to mention Mrs. Hoefer across the street.
I tell him Bill Berkson and Arthur Okamura
are my teachers.

These several selves that move one self around, thousands jiggling. It is so inappropriate to be unfound, whine around, hesitant, lock the window again, this body is dissipated. To accomplish, to learn, with thanks, to one's past history is brought up close. And for a while, with late spring's wild radish flower blooming past my window, the further shore is close, is here. I do not want to say he is dead yet because he has not yet come back, but my sadness for the missing comes recognised, is acceptable. Gone with the last look he questioned me with. Have you done this to me?

Indeed are they my forces or the forces I am within. That no children come from me to love. And I am this space in time, this focus, of articulation, that hears the bee buzz round and round.

I have large dreams of beautiful patterns.

Clouds over Indiana
And we are under them

Who even said I was a poet. Because I write
this down. I want bullet-like speed and precision
to show that this mind connects in ways of delight, and
also says truth way beyond this individual voice.
Thus I speak from the holy story, the ordinary story.
Thus I am married to the household gods, thus I aspire
to be the consort of heaven. Thus I am sad when the earth
is from me. We sleep together again. In no way will I
part from this union. And the sky who is my father
opens the world of the golden kingdom.

Even if I repeat what others say,
it becomes mine.

The famous Utah mountains embroidered in gold, russet
& pink.

LET YOUR SELF GO.

One thinks 'the obvious'. You say it sounds so obvious.
I wanted to do something I called writing.

I think you've done it
It's finished *now*.
It's a new map
in a delicate space
For what once was growing there.

ELKTON NATIO

Gregory Corso

The next morning, I think, did I dream all this? Returning late night from the party to instant sleep waking and talking with Ed on the phone.

Hark to the Herald. A Bolinas Beach morning early autumn 1977. Billy Burroughs Jr., Tasha Robbins, Gregory, myself. Just after 9am the market has opened and Gregory has bought a can of pineapple and a bottle of champagne. Just us on the beach. Look at him says Billy Burroughs Jr. He is the absolute greatest, we have to take care of him.

We are looking at my photo album from India. Hope Savage! (Hope Savage was a very early girlfriend of Corso.) She was my early mentor! Out comes the picture, a memento. He said I was "a good sort" in a letter I carried later to the mother of his daughter in Santa Fe. It's a Naropa summer. It's Sunday morning and everything is closed. Here's a glass of orange juice for you he says kindly. After I drink I find it's dosed with mescaline. A floating day, look look at those clouds. We are watching a grand and formal Japanese archery display. We go to Trungpa's house for cocktails and a talk. I'm standing by a pillar listening and I drop my glass. Oh look what boo boo you did Joanne, says Gregory loudly. You didn't have to answer him says Allen later. I said something foolish like "I support my corner of the house."

Gregory can read minds. He knows who's outside the door. Where the stash is hidden. And he goes right to the heart of beauty. He's sitting next to her, his arm around her, at home. Allen asks me to introduce Gregory and him at a Naropa summer reading. I want to give it some Cosmic Sizzle and talk about them as the White Lights of poetry. Gregory is terrifically angry and says white light! That's what you see when you die! I don't do the introduction.

You always know things will be lively, outspoken, truthful, around Gregory, provocative, on stage. Center stage for the muses.

2000

Interview with John Thorpe, *Convivio*

John Thorpe: Was a Buddhist sense of "right" or "noble" speech relevant to your writing?

Joanne Kyger: Right speech as I understand it is singing bullets connecting in the ear. A good ear differentiates the sounds very fast and precisely and connects positively to the heart. Buddhism calls that operation of cause and effect "Samsara." There really are no solid things. Samsara's like a big connected net of everything. It isn't "bad," it's relentlessly connecting and goes on forever and ever. There is no duality between "samsara" and "nirvana." The life and its compensations are of a piece, like protons and neutrons. Suffering is an illusion, because you extract it, make it up, out of the connecting net. People can equally find transmission and kinship there between all sorts of beings. But dig, I don't know even now what "being a Buddhist" would mean.

What do you think the Lotus symbolizes?

Well, I don't know what it "symbolizes." As far as I understand what a lotus is, a lotus comes out of the *muck*, and way down in the muddy muck, which is called the land, is this *root*. And this root comes out, and lo and behold it's got some anchorage, and it's got some green leaves around it too, and it looks innocuous enough. All of a sudden it brings forth this incredible, gracious, flat-formed petal—voilà!

In the O.E. Dictionary *the root of the English word "mind" is "memory," like Mnemosyne. How is your sense of what "mind" is?*

The mind is the big dome of everything that's going on in the world. I remember I took this acid trip when I went up to Yosemite Falls once with Peter Warshall, and up at the top I was totally terrified that I was going to slide off into Yosemite Falls. I had a purple crayon and I was drawing in this notebook and everything had *definite* auras, for instance green was red, and I got *mind* then. Lew Welch had died recently and he had told me that Buddhism teaches you how to *hone* the mind. You have this complete fantastic fantasy, universe, mind, dreaming, sleeping; in other words, you've *got* this mind. You're this human with enormous intelligence: so how does it become wieldy? Buddhism tells you how to sit with your mind, and hone it so you've got it inside some space of the breathing, plant, animal, world, surroundings . . . For example . . . the Dutch poets who were visiting here today had not seen a hummingbird before, and they thought it was a fantasy. They thought hummingbirds were a marvelous poetic being. So this one poet said, "Well now we've seen a hummingbird, where are your elves?" They visually hadn't seen this Californian phenomenon, this conglomeration of vegetation and trees, so it all became real as they say the first hummingbird they ever saw. A more open mind can bring out a little more space, a little more wonder, more congratulations, which is something I would like to do.

Do drugs help you open the mind, and/or are they allies in the life of poetry?

Poetry's an ally itself, and I think we all like to get together, you know. It's not like reading the *Wall Street Journal*. If I congratulate everything human and everything alive then I congratulate my own living. You too have this front porch that I'm sitting on and I can congratulate someone else sitting on this front porch. Specifically, we're drinking the vintage California wine and smoking the California smoke and we're living in this place and this day is congratulatory to us.

So you returned from East Asia to San Francisco and have pretty much stayed in northern California since?

Yes. My first book was set by the East Wind printers' linotype machine, and I oversaw the lines very carefully to be sure that the flow was moving across the page and that it accurately presented the passage of writing. Spicer would refer to this period (1957–64) as "completing my maze." The second book, *Places to Go*, got more adventuresome. I felt that language would move of its own accord.

Your word "passage" is interesting—to pass without stopping. The dictionary has "pass" as the past participle of the verb "pandere" derived from Greek "pandemos": "of all the people." Does that imply to you terrestrial exploration?

Not getting stuck in a singular state of mind. Cruising is something a poet has to do because she's always looking for her audience.

When you say "a place for her audience," that reminds me that, in Sumerian, the "brain" is supposedly identified with, or found in the sign of, an ear.

I think mostly ear. You can feel the editing that goes on in the ear. You pitch your tones environmentally to what's around you, and can speak ten or more languages if you really want to. Even the most repetitious cliché is like the Cyclades coming together. If you want to remind yourself of your oral tradition—the family history you take along with you—how do you want to feel akin to it? Ear is totally common and attractive. It's the only reason you want to listen.

Another word you refrain is "congratulatory." Does that mean to rejoice with the good fortune of another?

That's a necessary praise to bring, like seeing something that's appealing. I feel an outside language, of this good fortune that the sun is out and there are eight golden-crowned sparrows, perfect in their way. Congratulations! Going back to the muse, the muse can't be personal. The muse is like trying to hold the crystal, or hold the mirror, so that things get reflected back very quickly or immediately, and it's no personal problem for yourself.

Viswanatha Kaviraja's Sahityadarpana *(Bibliotheca India, Calcutta, 1875) describes the characteristics of poetic taste as "suavity, ardor, and evidence." Do those terms ring a bell?*

For *suavity*, I feel artful manifestation. What is going to intrigue your ear. He meant sweetness, perhaps. *Ardor*: a pan of coals. Passion. Get-it-right-type passion. And *evidence* would be to me commonplace detail, determining whether you can't believe it or can believe it. But, really, amigo, ideas are a dime a dozen. Ideas are something called our European structure of mind which sucks in the world, which our education has given us very freely and very generously. I don't want that. I want to see how you live *in* your environment or in your compassion for place. One thing I realized teaching at Naropa Institute this summer, as the class was reading Jaime de Angulo, was that I was really trying to get people over to this space where they have some animal-spirit connection. To realize that the tree is in a simultaneous breath with ourselves, and it's not a *difference* of consciousness. The tree is talking directly to me, rather than the tree is a likeness like some other metaphorical likeness. Some of the students really had "Bambi" identifications and I wanted to suggest a more *warmed-up* feeling, past some objective sense of nature, swooshing into it, allowing the fox to have a personality, responding to tree speech with human speech as one continuity.

Which Western schooling calls "anthropomorphism, projection, sympathetic magic, pathetic fallacy," etc.

Fuck *that*, man. You see the little bamboo grove over there? Now watch, when I breathe, I'm going to breathe over there in it and congratulate it. *Hmmm. I want you to feel good, bamboo. And that's all right, you'll feel good. We'll listen to you for a while, bamboo.* What do you see in the grove?

The bamboo are stirring gently in a rustling pattern, bowing slightly, opening their branches to the wind. I feel the excitement but it's very familiar, like the resonant sound of the word "bamboo." That reminds me, in one poem you said "I speak from the holy story, the ordinary story."

Joseph and his family, that's all. It's the same human story that happens. Magic is the *warmth* of human beings reaching and deciding that the animistic, or the circumstances of their life, have some importance. When they have *great* importance you become overwhelmed by them. You say, yeah, this means this.

Do you have any particularly familiar local spirit-companions?

Always. The hummingbird, blue jay, the great blue heron. Mostly harbinger spirits. My plant spirits are a little different, they are heavy spirit-changers. The amanita mushroom. Marijuana is another harbinger. And peyote of course which doesn't come from here.

Are your animal-spirit companions and psychoactive herbs related to witchcraft too?

Definitely. But now animism has negative connotations. "Good" or "bad" doesn't apply. It's what the people in the mountains are practicing. The shaman's traditional responsibility is to activate the strength of words, because sound is transformational and transformation manifests in terms of power. A shaman goes to *another* world to find cures, she has to be very very careful to get there and to get back.

Who or what are you learning most from these days?

I've tried to do a kind of trance thing called Moonwriting, and found out that it's eidetically easier for me to move from right to left, curiously. I get information from dreams, but that's exactly what it is—information. I learn from anthropologists, and from people who still live in relation to animal-spirit companions.

Do you think human additions to nature have been harmful on the whole?

Yeah. That's a terrible thing to say, how could I amend that? Do you mean the Transamerica Building or what, exactly? The hardest thing I have to deal with is about how humans are unnecessary in terms of existing here at all, except that more people come out of more people. It's a totally klutzed-up landscape and that's the most pain I feel. When humans never get aware of that, when they get more and more demanding, from the state or the church or whatever. The land doesn't need us one bit. And I hope the land feels well. If you feel well toward the land you're on, it feels well back toward you. I'm doubtful of substitutions and amazed it still grows roses these days.

Then how would you like to live if you could have your dream come true?

Just like now.

1983

Full of Birds in the First

soft rain of the year, gold and white crown
sparrows, one rufus sided
and three brown
towhees, the energetically scratching fox
sparrow, the ten members
of the quail flock, the remaining song sparrow

whose mate got ate by the black cat
last week, anna hummingbird blur, red
finch, the pair of red
shafted flickers, and those noisy scrub
jays we always chase out
of the garden by clapping our hands,

the mockingbirds, the flock
of robins in the pine looking at the bright
berries of the cotoneaster soon to make them drunk
kinglets, wren tits, they're all here now

in this rain, in the gather dome

october 1993
for Jack Collom

March 6 '86

The large mixed flock of sparrows have been gone for several weeks now a few small flocks of white crowns*

The wildlife photography of the "Roots" (sp?) from Africa.

*a few gold crowns too

3/17

Last few DAYS 2 Bewicks wrens trying to build a nest in the eves of the front porch

But don't like it when we sit there

April 6 · Monday '86

hundreds of Cedar Wax wings in the Eucalyptus grove by Bob Scott's.

June 10 · Tuesday '86

Currently at the Kitchen window feeder:

2 very fat Tohee

2 Song Sparrows

Phoebe around & House finch in garden today ~ mockin bird off in the distance.

Don cutting grass discovers Garter Snake w/mouth around half swallowed Mouse

Out the window October 27. on the verge of the first rain) '87
(light showers a week ago)

mocking bird
flicker pecking ground
Anna Humming bird
gold crown · white crown
Fox sparrow · song sparrow

September 22, 1989. Friday

Can you imagine: Just like the swallows of Capistrano: The flock of White Crown & Gold Crown arrived. on the button yesterday just like they did last year Sept. 21 : Fall Equinox

In the garden still waiting to jump into feeding station under window ~ which has not been used until they left last April.

A strange visitor this morning along with Scrub jay is a black head Stellar jay

Robert Creeley introduction to a Joanne Kyger reading in Buffalo, April 2, 1982

The first time I was ever granted audience with the First Lady of Poetry was in the smoky recesses of The Place somewhere in the hinterland of San Francisco's equivalent to the Lower East Side, sometime in the late '50s. She was known, I believe, as Miss Kids—due to the fact that she so addressed her company in amongst the rush of much other stuff she was saying. Lew Welch has immortalized that period of her incredible life with a play no less called "Thirty Thirty," p.122–23 of his HOW I WORK AS A POET . . .

She remarks that she fell in with poets circa 1957, and that company included Harold Dull, George Stanley, John Wieners, Ebbe Borregaard, and Richard Brautigan—in short, the people who were picking up on Jack Spicer long before the rest of us had even read him. One could stop here to do a whole trip on Great Moments in Literary History, but let us hasten on. There is no poet with more whimsically tough a mind, no one who moves faster in a seeming offhand attention and purpose. That is, she's the best of the West, at least in this easterner's imagination. For example, she had the wit to rewrite the Odyssey from Penelope's so-called point of view, and she writes of a Buddhism I for one have longed for, viz not more of that puritan intellectualism and things to do today, but an up front seat "utmost uproars of emotion" kind of Coyote. I can dig it . . .

So here's your own chance folks. "Kyger, Kyger, Burning Bright, In the Forests of the Night". . . Blake sure knew, and so does Joanne Elizabeth Kyger—once and for all. Please welcome her.

PREVIOUS PAGES: From Joanne Kyger's bird notebooks.

Interview with Dale Smith & Michael Price, *Jacket*

Dale Smith: Your poetry is very much in your mouth. You hear the voice thinking and exploring, revealing . . .

Joanne Kyger: It's a physical voice, yes. I think that's the best you can do sometimes, trying to "score" it as closely as you can on the page. I'm always amazed that this isn't taught more. How to translate the voice to the page, to get the little subtleties of breath and tone, or change of tone or character emphasis.

There's one really good essay that I've never been able to find again, I think by Williams. He says, okay, let's get this all down: a period has three breath stops; a comma has a breath stop, a semi-colon, a breath stop and a half. Empty space means nothing goes on but breathing until you get to the next word, etc. You're scoring your reading. Otherwise you follow this boring convention of the straight left-hand margin, a kind of cookie-cutter block stamp.

DS: You've mentioned before your daily practice of writing in a journal.

Yes, and in this daily writing, you don't have to think of it as "poetry," you don't have to think at all about what "kind" of writing you're doing. You're writing some kind of un-self-conscious open utterance, being as clear as you can, or as muddled as you want. You're not writing for anybody. It's spontaneous.

DS: It seems definitely un-self-conscious. Because when you sit down to write a poem and think, okay, this poem's got to be this or that, that's when poems really get bogged down. They're most free when you can step out and not be self-conscious.

Right. Know how to step "out" of what you call a form; wake up. Keep word energy flowing. That's why I love travel writing. When people on trips write about what's happening, they're out of their own familiar habitat and experiencing something new, strange, awful. That can produce very fresh and inspiring writing. Very human, very vulnerable.

DS: You're very vulnerable when it's a place you don't know. Do you write for anybody in particular?

I think there's a kind of address that goes on all the time, especially to your peers in poetry. Once you've published, you do realize someone is hopefully going to read your words.

DS: Do you ever publish your journals?

Yes. For example, *Phenomenological* was a journal written in the Yucatan and was part of an "assignment" in a series of chapbooks called "The Curriculum of the Soul." A series published by the late John Clarke and Al Glover based on a list of "topics" by Charles Olson. As a form it contained many different kinds of writing: poetry, biography, quotations, dreams, travel observations, historical data about the Yucatan Mayans, conversations, etc.

DS: Did you know Olson, did you work with him?

I met him in 1965 at the Berkeley Poetry Conference. He also came out to San Francisco to participate for a month on an experimental television project at KQED. I got to know him a lot better then. Bill Brown was also working with the project. Bill had transcribed and published through his press Coyote Press, Olson's filibuster talk phenomenon at the '65 Conference. I remember him as being a brilliant and continuous conversationalist, his ear so keen.

Of course Joe Dunn had given me *Projective Verse* to read in 1957. I really studied it. I'd come out of the University of California at Santa Barbara studying Wittgenstein and Heidegger. I liked looking at what "thoughts" were about. I hadn't heard anyone trying to talk about writing or poetry that had a language, an articulation. I read *Projective Verse* over and over again, trying to "fathom" or absorb it. There was a field, an energy, energy on the page. The page itself was an energy source, and words and ideas were transmitted to it. As quick as ideas arrived they should be transformed into this field.

Robert Duncan, Snyder, and Ginsberg were articulating their own poetics. But for me, I could really understand how the page could start to hold these "energies."

Michael Price: That's interesting that you say that, because for me, just holding a book of Olson's has that energy. I've noticed that with your books too. I'm just getting to know them. The same with Philip Whalen. There's something about the presence of even the book itself.

Well, yes, the pages certainly look alive. I mean it's so boring to pick up a book of poetry and see that left-handed margin going evenly up and down the page like a little platoon of soldiers.

MP: It's almost like running up and down a staircase over and over again, instead of wandering everywhere.

DS: That's about the power of observation. Olson magnified it. I mean it was so ingrained with him. That Bibliography on America for Ed Dorn. *He says something like "just go study barbed wire."*

He didn't start writing poetry until his forties, so he had a very well-developed intellect, and was a wide reader. A person willing to go beyond the usual bounds of the Greek-Roman Empire, Judeo-Christian inheritance.

DS: What do you mean, as you say in one of your poems, "Me is memory . . . take me out, take me out."

You are composed of all of the ideas of yourself, so "you" are your memory, so "you" are your history. How you solidify a "me."

"Take me out" means take "me" out, so "I" can view someone else's memory. If you are going to try and go out to another time and history to tell someone else's story, you have to drop that "me" behind.

DS: What do you mean by "architecture of your lineage?"

Who your teachers are; how did you learn the architecture of your page, become aware of the "structure" of your thinking and the books in your life. Robert Duncan was especially important to me when I was young as he presented the "religion" of the household. He's a person who just unabashedly made a wonderful, magical home. Unlike Spicer who lived a lonely life in dreary apartment rooms. How do you make your household? How do you keep it together, to live a life that is balanced with beauty? A place to put your bookshelves. But not get tied down too much. The rucksack revolution of the Beat Generation was to be able to know how to get on the road too. You had to know how to earn your living, at a job that you didn't confuse with your "identity," but gave you the economics to travel, and time off to write.

DS: The architecture of "me." That's why I was wondering about the "me." Poetry does something to that "me" because it's "you" but not "you." "Well I myself, am not myself" you say. It's a distance, but it's very close. It's an inhabited distance of revelation. There's something, ultimately, in good poems that you just can't control. It just happens, and you're always stunned and surprised when you've done something really good, you see something you didn't expect to see.

That's when you understand that words have their own independent existence. They say what they want to. Like Spicer saying you are just the medium, the funnel for the words to go through. They have their own lineage, returning through you. The magic syllables, seed syllables.

1997

from *Lo & Behold: Household and Threshold on California's North Coast*

1986

All channels covering the demise of the space shuttle people.

I stroll on one foot through the farther edges of my domestic geography
The other one is broken.

All roads closed into town, flooding at the bridge, convergence zone
                    of tropical and northern storms.
The real people of the wind and rain arrive
      sounding like Tangos of Grace
            for the rest of the afternoon

The eyes vibe with familiarity upon the pink double petaled camellia
So sitting here asking—where was the architecture of beauty 200 years ago?
     not a ruin in sight.

Finally we have stepped aside—and filled the empty space
      with the soft real buzzing of all the busy pollinators.
           Far away from the low tide ear on the reef.
  Inside the narrative you understand the longer history,
               past the tragedy of the present.

  "Milarepa tried to warn us.
   Robert Herrick tried to warn us.
   Philip Whalen tried to warn us. But
   we went ahead & had that 4th cup of coffee. Yuck!"
                    —Shao

"How could so large a man have such glistening little rabbit turds for eyes."

Ah, moon, the jewel of perfect wisdom, is found full, in late night
western window.

"Civilizations are never lost.
History is a continuum—an intermingling web of peoples, built like temples
one over the other."

Don uses his chain saw at Sonoma Mountain Zen Center
I see the live ones in the evening breeze
waving up and down
Bay Tree
byeeeee bye

Dharma says that one thing depends upon another,
is intimately related to everything else.

When I walk my mind goes in a million directions
Now I walk in peace
With each step I create a warm breeze
with each step a lotus blooms (isn't that asking an awful lot?)
—Thich Nhat Hanh

Tsunami Festival

Last night on the mesa overlook, our little coast community evacuated.
A small party. Fire engines downtown. Standing, sitting on the cliff watching
in the dark the calm ripples of the bay.
What happened to that 600 mph wave anyway.

Candidates night at the utility district. Our government.
Is all about water and septic tanks and second units.
And yawn, why is She running, she's so Vague.

The "thrown in" style of writing,
like the Tea House style of flower arrangement.
After the formal structure is learned, the casual can happen.
Hopefully becoming an "invisible" art.

Can man live without conflict? Can man live without profit?
Can man live without the fresh water river otter I just saw?
It's a political responsibility to know the history of where you are.

Practice not discussing the faults of others
　　　　and not praising yourself, while abusing others.

Suddenly it's time for the first Fog Festival.
It's Fogust. Nude arm fog bathing.

　　　　　Named their village after the water they drink.

1987

Rain and gusty wind. A house burns down.

Chogyam Trungpa dies at his home in Halifax, April 13, 1987.
He is placed in meditation position, seed syllables on parts of his body.
Cremated and a rainbow arises.

Don cuts and shapes the trees around Suzuki Roshi's stone stupa at Sonoma Mountain.

Once again I am in this position of being at a poetry reading, at the library
waiting, getting ready to listen and trying not
to Bolt out the door with total Loathing of the situation
What I want to know, Is he telling the truth?

The funky Cadillac convertible, driven in the July 4th parade by a blind surfer,
is found in lagoon mouth full of sand and beer cans. And somehow is driven away.

The Harmonic Convergence has pseudo deer-clad Pocahontas white girls doing new age
Indian dances. On the top peak of the coast range. Very fake.

Sell $40 worth of apples from our trees to the people's store downtown.
Flocks of Golden-crowned Kinglets eating thistle seeds.

In a fishing boat under the Golden Gate Bridge, catch two salmon.

Do you want to be a bird admired? Gold-crown and White-crown have returned.
This time of year has just turned green.

A Mariachi band for the Christmas party downtown at the community center.
We exchange our new color tv set four times, over the hill, to get one that works.

Blustery, windy, rainy. I think I lost my flashlight. Enjoy! our Wild America.

1988

Little bit by little bit, we fix the day.

First day of April—   April fool
    full moon,
        Passover Seder,
            Good Friday.
Garlands of herring eggs on the low-tide beach.

It was so boring, I stayed up until 4am reading it.
    You could hear every sentence clank into place.

I dream Trungpa tells me how much the poets, like Allen Ginsberg, mean to him.

After the Blue Coral Reef reading, we are served sushi in the aquarium,
 and all the fish look at us.

Holy matrimony, lives entwined, in Beverly Hills. I wish I had something for the ants.

"This is my favorite ex-wife."

Where the flow of consciousness goes. Hi! here's the fly.
I babysit Birdy, the red and green parrot.

Where do you live?
Have you got a calendar? Let me show you . . .
Brown towhee makes the first morning sound.

"I want the superb with hot and cold running water
    in the center of a vast impenetrable wilderness." —PW

"Of course we need a plan that will solve the problems of the documented
136 houses on the mesa that have septic failures. But at the cost of $5 million dollars? The inefficient enormity of this current plan frankly disgusts me."

The dominant culture's voraciousness is so overwhelming.

On the pier in a small waterfront restaurant I hear about the leaping board parable from the sham teacher. It's an actual ride. One simply mounts or clutches this board while wearing one's white robes and it starts bucking and jumping around. This is a religious phenomenon.

Seasonal supper of crab, oysters, chanterelles, baguette, and champagne.

His poetry is essentially a commentary on "language."
  Someone just ran out the door and down the steps.

  "Dead listeners cannot be retrieved."

Facing west, out to sea,
                    where am I going to go, what can I do?

          Be aware of this clarity!
Singular call of the Gold-crown bestirs lethargic apathetic senses
     from the soul's desultory awareness.

Sound of surf through the open front door. And a fishy soup smell.

  South of us this year was fire, snow, sleet, huge winds, and earthquakes.

Interview with David Meltzer, James Brook, Steve Jones, and Marina Lazzara, from *San Francisco Beat: Talking with the Poets*

David Meltzer: How has San Francisco poetry scene changed?

Joanne Kyger: Well, I don't go in that much. There's not a real center of poetry anymore, for various reasons. I think of the readings of the late sixties, where we had 500 to 1,000 people at a reading. Poetry was the news, the cultural news, and I don't think we've had this kind of energy, these kind of voices for a while—certainly, rock music took over a lot of social commentary . . . The Language school I felt was a kind of an alienating intellectualization of the energies of poetry. It carried it away from the source. It may have been a housecleaning from confessional poetry, but I found it a sterilization of poetry. On the other hand, spoken word poetry is an identification with the voice energy.

DM: There are two distinct operations: the writing and the performing of the poem.

James Brook: Getting back to your practice, Joanne. We talked a little about your devotion to poetry and Buddhism and vice-versa. Is there a way that you approach poetry, your perspective on writing as an act—the way you sit down and decide or not decide to start or how things are to be arranged on the page?

Accepting that the mind is OK as it is. I don't have an official Buddhist teacher. I go through phases of practicing meditation on a daily scale and then not doing it for a long time and then going back to it. But you know it's not practice that's ultimately rejected—you just get out of the tempo of doing it. You find that when you finally sit or practice meditation everything about you slows down. Your "content" becomes more accessible and . . . it goes back to Trungpa's dictum, "first thought best thought." So what arises comes out. And then the next thing arises, and so you put that down. You trust that your mind is shapely and that existence has a flow of its own. It's not trying to restructure your thinking to come to conclusions. A hierarchical sense of where you are starts to fade away. In its simplest focus, that's how I see it.

DM: Let's talk about your relationship with Philip Whalen's work and presence. How has he taught you—directly or indirectly—poetry and Buddhism? Or has he not? Has it been just reading his books and hanging out with him?

Phil would always just say just keep on writing. You have to get beyond the point where this is a good poem and that's a bad poem. Philip's playfulness showed the playfulness of the mind—he showed how different voices come in and they all have equal value and not just one voice is you. The equality of thought . . . there's a good deal of humor with Philip.

DM: It's an interesting way of being serious. You often spin a poem with humor . . .

So do you . . .

DM: I know. That's why I like reading your poetry. [Laughter.] I like the notion of the poem as a field of play; it's not necessarily some monumental Gothic cathedral you can't get off your head.

I think that *Just Space*, the book that Black Sparrow put out in the '80s, is essentially a kind of daybook, at times attempting to keep a longer narrative going, a story. It essentially is asking, "What does the day offer?"—in terms of the myriad sources of its particulars.

JB: Could we step through the books now as markers in an autobiography?

OK. This was my first book. Don Allen published *The Tapestry and the Web* in 1965. I said that when I was in Japan I didn't have any real feeling where I was at in terms of writing. I came back to San Francisco, and Don wanted to publish a book. *The Tapestry and the Web* starts with the first poem that I felt was successful—written in 1958, when I was living in San Francisco and going to the Spicer/Duncan group. The early parts are San Francisco poems and poems written in Japan. It uses Homer's *Odyssey* as a structural outline, a trip into a life. I had read Joseph Campbell's *The Hero with a Thousand Faces*. You get an idea of narrative in terms of myth—Campbell expanded the idea of what myth was about into the currents of your own life. It's the oldest narrative that I could find on how to look at your life and how to look at this larger story. Homer was useful for me. Somebody asked me a few years ago, "Who are these gods and goddesses you talk about all the time?" I said they're around. But they were a lot more around in the late fifties and the sixties. It was a kind of concurrent mythology. Certainly, Robert Duncan used them a lot. It was part of a psychological family that belonged to poetry, and you could call upon them and turn them into voices, and they acted on the impulses and dramatics of your own life. And put you into the big story. Poetry wants to be inside the big story. Part of the voice of the big story. I don't hear too much about the gods and goddesses, anymore. Well, the goddesses are there with New Age religion. Demeter's around a lot. And Persephone. I don't hear a lot about Athena.

Steve Jones: Well, in pop culture there are those two TV series, Hercules *and* Xena.

Wow, I love that. In Robert Graves's *The Greek Myths* you begin to realize these myths are reinterpreted in a lot of different places—one person or god turns into another. What was the other book that came out at that time?

DM: The White Goddess*?*

The White Goddess, right. Although since the White Goddess is a woman and the muse herself, she could never write poetry. Which I thought was a real cop out! [Laughter.]

DM: The Spicer/Duncan group did place a heavy emphasis on muse and on certain forms of inspiration or reception . . .

Lew Welch got so mad at them because they would always talk about "The Poem." "The Poem." Capital T, capital P.

DM: And all Lew wanted was to have people in the bar understand his poetry, not Poetry.

Exactly.

DM: "Inspirare" means "the in-breath," "to be breathed through." Something breathes through you, and you exhale it, and there's a poem on the page, and you say, hmm, what's this? These aren't my hands. That brings up an interesting question: who writes the poem? You were talking about how the mind is writing a poem like in meditation, the mind's activity to project itself. But who's the mind? Is the mind you?

You've already inherited it. You've inherited paper. You've inherited a tradition. If you decide to enter into that tradition, that lineage, you already find yourself a part of it. You are already there. You are looking at the mind, or the mind is just looking. "Who" writes down what the mind says? I think the words have a mind of their own. You must discover that words want to put themselves down. I think after a while you're like a musician: you play your own tune. It's like a set piece. Without much effort. But it's dangerous. You could write the same poem over and over again. You find a form, an ear, a relationship of self to the world. You just have to keep yourself open because then this wonderful poem could come along and knock your socks off.

DM: So it's not Invasion of the Body Snatchers*?*

SJ: Definitely not that!

DM: Joanne *was published by . . .*

Angel Hair.

DM: In terms of form, that book was very different from The Tapestry and the Web.

Right. I wrote it in 1970. In the early seventies there was a whole pared-down identity number that went on. *Joanne: A Novel from the Inside Out*—with the idea that the plot's so huge, all you have is this small space of notational nuggets. You're so busy living the novel that you don't have any time to write it down. So you just have little comments, hits in the middle of the day.

DM: The footnotes to the novel.

It was just called *Joanne*. It didn't have any author name on it. As though it had written itself.

DM: Just a black-and-white photograph of you on the cover. Could we talk about people like Berrigan and that younger group of poets associated with the East Coast?

The so-called second-generation New York School. I met them when I lived in New York City for nine months. That's when I met Anne Waldman and Lewis Warsh. I had published Lewis in *Wild Dog* when I was editor. That was a magazine Ed Dorn started in Idaho, then it came out to San Francisco. In 1965, Anne, Lewis, and Ted had come out for the poetry conference in Berkeley. This was a major confluence of what was the New American Poetry at that time. It was fraught with political and social excitement. I went to New York around 1967, and I met Anne, Michael Brownstein, and Lewis and Ted. I didn't like New York at all. I was too much a West Coast person.

DM: I know some of the influences then, but who influences you today? Who do you read?

Well, I read my contemporaries still. I don't really curl up with a book of poetry. I love to read, and I read a lot. But I find that poetry is best read out loud for me. To catch the ear first. Some books of poetry are constructed so they are readable but I'm . . . well, often everything is lined up on the left-hand margin and the form looks the same all the time. I need a plot. I need to have something going on. So I can get in touch with the writer. I appreciate that. Philip Whalen I can read. Anne Waldman, Anselm Hollo, Ed Sanders, Alice Notley. I feel lonesome if I sit down all alone with a book of poetry. It makes me anxious. I read it a little while, and then I want to go write my own.

1998

· a reliquary.
Joe gave me this scab

JOE BRAINARD

We're going to spend the afternoon together at his loft in the Soho. It's his first loft, and I haven't seen it. I'm in New York to do a poetry reading, Z Press's Kenward Elmslie has just published The Wonderful Focus of You. It's February 1980. ~~Lynn and Bill are living in the Hamptons for a year off from Bolinas~~.

As Joe and I walk to his loft from Kenward's on Greenwich, where I'm staying, I try to recognize where I am. The 'Soho' has emmerged since I lived there in 1966 in a loft on Grand and Green underneath Jack Smith the madman filmaker of Flaming Creatures. I don't recognize a thing. [In Joe's loft we get high, with very strong grass and a bloody Mary.

Then he brings out a box of beautiful jewelry he has acquired, authentic and tasteful. Choose something for yourself, he tells me. Pieces from India, China, Africa. I take an American Southwest turqoise and heishe bead necklace. ~~It's~~ a real treasure.

Then he says do you want to take a Quaalude. I say sure, ~~he thinks it's a good idea~~, I've never tried one. So I swallow the quaalude and have another bloody mary. Joe says do you want to make a collage out of these little pieces of colored paper? I try to, but I'm all rubbery. It's certainly a lot harder than it looks, to be casual. So then we lay down on the bed and listen to music. A much safer place to be. What was the music? It must have been just right, because everything Joe did was so considerate. I can see us from an ariel view, looking as if we were strapped ~~in~~ for a rocket launch.

After a while we ~~go~~ down meet Kenward ~~on the street~~ and go to dinner. Everything is vastly relaxed and amusing. There is a careful navigation of words and phrases.

~~I think later~~, is Joe showing me how he spends his day? ~~Oh if I could have just~~ made a collage.
whish

Memorial Day May 29. Boy I wish I could have made a collage.

January 7

Dear Joe
                    your friendship really
'treasured' as   the most glamorous
and generous. Back in the past I Remember

The Acid Trip with Joe in Bo
when we sat under the french broom
and looked at the teeny peapod seeds,
    the shinning eucalyptus leaves
   oily and flashing in the sun.
Oh, the most awful thing, you say,
Bill scratched up this dirt and there was
cement underneath, I think it's his
septic tank . . .
              Childlike, innocent
first giddy beauty. The natural
haphazard casual toss
     of offerings from the beach
shore line harmoniously positioned
together in tiny framed collages.
                        Memory is still alive
        but altered, edited, what else
did we do that day. Touched by your wondering
truthful ministry.
       It was before I got my house.
You never came here again.

May 26, 1994

It's different here now having been

to the other coast and returned to hit the sharp

edge of newness—linear lines of old old roar
pouring in over it. New, old, just habitat words
for this existence.

Dick Gallup called yesterday at 6pm to say Joe
Brainard had died three hours ago.

No words, just acceptance for now.

June 4 Saturday

Postcard from Joe

He is lying in bed
The Angel and Devil are fighting
over his body
'Heaven and Heck'
March '93
'I want
to insert myself
into your thoughts'.

The minister of short sermons
of enlightenment: I remember
we got stuck
in the Buffalo airport's rain
you and I
supplying glamour
for each other
Finally you asked
'Know any games?'

June 25

'A Joe Brainard's Trip Box for Joanne 1971'

Found objects ready for new memory
A ground down Tareyton cigarette butt
  which the lips of JB must have touched
A letter from 1887
A zipper
Treasures I gave away
A hand printed card: Short Story
A very sad thing
Happened at the Zoo.
Judy, Bill's mother, Be-
came very sick and
died.
'Compliments of the author.'
'A clap of Thunder.'
Prayer to Our Mother of Perpetual Help
Pins: Bean Spasms
    No More Draft . . . .

'And HAPPY TRIPING!

or is it TRIPPING?

And MANY MORE!

Love, Joe'

FRAMES

for Joanne Kyger

This landscape of hers is structure, like glass
or some great monument

super as it is hers
and for water we used rain.

A life you involved around flowers
was the tokens, enormous as they were grand
some in the morning (you wept)

the night crept for you like tissue
gathered in the dawn cloth,
and the rest?
they watched amazed that such a life

Your completion in the dream was stately
Tall, thin, you took the glass

broken where she sipped, the lips opened to you
and everywhere getting through the land

Light.

1. the sleeves flap in the dance you do to shame us

2. the hesitant love mounting
as in New York we miss you

and you go.

for Joanne
love,
Anne

Questions for Joanne Kyger from Anne Waldman, from *Civil Disobediences: Poetics and Politics in Action*

Anne Waldman: Since we have been staying and working together here in the Mexican city of Pátzcuaro, a place you know, it would be interesting to ask about your recent book, Pátzcuaro *(Blue Millennium Press, Bolinas, 1999). Were the pieces and poems in there extracted from or embellished upon an earlier journal? What was the time frame?*

Joanne Kyger: My first trip to Pátzcuaro in 1986 with Donald Guravich was so pleasing we've returned many times since—this is our fifth visit. We stayed for three months during the winter of 1990–91. I wanted to feel what it was like to really live there, shop, cook, settle in. I always kept a journal but not a lot of "poems" arrived.

So on our visit to Pátzcuaro from December 17, 1997, to January 26, 1998, I wanted to attempt to compose some words that were more "precise." I approached this formally at a certain time every day, and excerpted journal entries I had written over the past weeks—a collage portrait of events, including dreams that seemed prescient. I gave myself lots of space on the page using a 9 × 12 water color sketchbook. I did this periodically over our 40-day stay and the poems in the book resulted.

December is a time of celebration for the local Virgin of Health, de la Salud, who is much revered all over the state of Michoacán. This is followed by the celebration for the Virgin Guadalupe, the Empress of Mexico. The outpouring of worship and petitioning given to these two deities moved me deeply. Worshippers cared in a deep and fundamental spiritual way, they *believed*.

So there were these currents of worship running along with the everyday necessities of buying and selling food, clothing, local handicrafts, all happening in the same location at the cathedral. And then there was me, the writer trying to connect, with daily living, the weather, dreams. Margaret Drabble popped up in a dream soon after I had arrived. I was unfamiliar with her work but read it after I returned to California. Humorous, wry, domestic, English. I took what dreams presented as information.

Then I found what sketchy historical pieces that were available of pre-conquest Pátzcuaro and added those. The destruction of the culture and libraries during the conquest of Mexico leaves much of the history conjectural. But the Purépecha, the native speakers of the area, have survived and live there today in villages around Lake Pátzcuaro.

When I moved to Bolinas in 1969, a small town on the coast north of San Francisco, where I still live, I experienced the cultural emptiness of the place. The Coast Miwok were no longer inhabitants, as a result of the gold invasion of the last century, and had left no edifices. I realized that everything in the small cottage in which I lived had been brought from somewhere else. But where was *here*. I knew that at one time in California's early and short history it had been part of Mexico. I started to think "north" and "south," this hemisphere.

After that first trip to Mexico I understood how little "Americans" actually know about what lies south of the border, the United States of Mexico. How in terms of the history of indigenous tribal movement, there is no border. How a sense of who I am culturally, geographically, has to do with the heritage of this continent.

Perhaps you could speak about your long relationship to Mexico—as a writer. What drew you here initially? What was the occasion?

Over the past 30 years I have visited Mexico 10 times. My first trip was to San Cristobal de las Casas in 1972 where I saw Mayan tribal living, ladino culture and some of the many different geographies of which Mexico is comprised. On a subsequent trip to San Cristobal I wrote a series of poems called "News from Maya Land," published in *The Wonderful Focus of You* (Z Press, 1980). The ancestral spirits of the Mayan people have never left and one sees how lightly and with what a delicious scramble conquest Christianity lays over their religion.

Visiting the Yucatan Peninsula in 1985 I kept a journal which was published as a part of Charles Olson's Curriculum of the Soul Series, titled *Phenomenological*. This amazing country of pyramids and civilizations of antiquity showed me how little we of this hemisphere understood our own geographical history. Trips to Oaxaca revealed further monumental pyramids, ruins, and culture.

Before 1972 in order to understand where my "roots" were as an "American" human being, I had thought "east" and "west." Living in Japan for four years, from 1960 to 1964 with a six-month trip to India (*The Japan and India Journals*), I got some sense of the religion and culture of the "east." Then realizing I needed to know my "old world" origins, my Atlantic crossing roots, I spent nine months visiting the cities and museums of Europe in 1966–67, ending with a year in New York City.

You have strong political feelings concerning NAFTA, the tense situation in Chiapas, the fate of the indigenous people here in Michoacán. What is your current view of these endangered cultures?

There is no denying there is striking poverty in Mexico and NAFTA seems to add to it. Simply put, NAFTA has had horrible consequences for a vast majority of Mexicans—the working poor, small farmers, etc. It is an organization that is the brainchild of the multi-nationals and corporate government under the guise of "free trade." What little was left of the positive results of the Mexican Revolution has been seriously undermined. Safety, environmental and wage laws have been eroded. An easy example would be the exponential growth of maquiladoras along the Mexican border, and the subsequent rise in pollution and union busting that accompanied that growth. Farther south, in poor states like Oaxaca and Chiapas, it is the dumping of cheap corn on the market by U.S. agricultural business that is one of the biggest threats. The small farmer simply cannot compete with a product that results from mega-use of pesticides, herbicides, and chemical fertilizers, that is highly mechanized and grown on huge tracts of land. Corn, for tortillas, is a major staple in Mexican diet. Corn and coffee growing are one of the main triggers for the Zapatista uprising in Chiapas. That and the opening up of Ejido, or communal land, to privatization. First NAFTA pushes farmers into a position where they cannot compete, then it gives them the opportunity to sell out when they are desperate. Ejido land was common land owned by indigenous villages and tribes which could not be sold, was handed down through generations. Now big business, big landowners are buying up these small farms and the small farmer is where he was before the revolution—working for the wealthy. About 10 percent of the population of Mexico owns over 41 percent of the wealth. The army in Chiapas seems to support that wealthy but powerful minority. Unions are basically wiped out when large companies impose their wage scale. And it is the indigenous people, the humans on the lowest scale of the economy who continually suffer.

Today in downtown Pátzcuaro we passed a group of farmers who had closed the Banca Serfin on the main plaza with a sign draped across it saying in effect that the farmers of Pátzcuaro should be helped, but the bankers are only interested in helping themselves. The small farmers of Michoacán are losing their land in much the same way the small farms of the U.S. lost theirs to "big business" and the banks.

Along the same lines, "Globalization" is a real threat to the support of "endangered cultures" as it means competitive prices, which in turn means going to countries where goods can be produced at the lowest wages and natural resources harvested at the lowest prices. Which is what the bottom scale of Mexican wages are all about as an "emerging economy." The current president, Ernesto Zedillo, in the continuing political rhetoric of his party stresses the "right" of Mexico to develop a competitive global economy and lauds "the inhabitants of old Mayan towns working in the new garment factories established in the Yucatán; rural migrants from southern Mexico finding jobs in the gigantic maquiladora plants of Tijuana and Juárez," etc. Yuk.

How do you see the "economics" of poetry in the current Distraction Culture?

When I was a young poet in the late '50s and studying informally with Jack Spicer and Robert Duncan, and reading the Beat writers like Kerouac, Ginsberg, Snyder, Whalen, etc. I was aware that these writers and poets were outside the then current University or academy scene. The "New American Poets" as Don Allen called the collection that introduced them to the public at large, were not beholden to the University for their living and were therefore able to write as they wished. They were part of a generation that made their livelihood by working often at "blue collar" jobs—merchant seaman, forestry service, post office, warehouses, etc. (Robert Duncan typed manuscripts.) This style of earning income allowed freedom from the establishment's "man in the gray flannel suit." One could save money and take time off to write, paint, and live a modest existence, but with the company of others in small groups and communities of like-minded people. I worked variously as a secretary in a bookstore and as a part time office person.

Poets were always poor in income but hopefully great in spirit and were published by the small presses that came into being in order to print them.

I haven't seen that "outlaw" tradition in some time. More poets now seem to be published by university presses, speak at "conferences," earn attractive incomes, have "high" standards of living, seem rather bland and formulaic, get stuck in graduate programs writing about poets that were "rebels." There is nothing "wrong" with this, one needs to make a living, but it is often a dependent relationship. The whole approach to "right livelihood" is a constant consideration. Poets who actually make a decent livable income from just writing is probably nil these days, and fortunately there are some teaching jobs that are free from academic restraints.

The whole occupation of poet, if it does exist as an identity in the current society, is one that has to do with a spiritual, cultural practice of words, and can't be "bought."

I've noticed you always carry a small notebook noting the exact times and locations of particular incidents and events, great and small. You spoke of your journal practice in our "Luminous details" workshop here. Could you reiterate some of that?

I keep a small daily notebook for jotting down the endless "things to do" list. The day's date at the top of the page. This is the notebook that accompanies me wherever I go during the day. When traveling I find it especially useful to jot down any information, names, phrases, directions, thoughts that enter the mind. Otherwise they're gone, whether trivial or important. It solidifies all the ephemeral of daily interaction, observations.

My larger spiral-bound notebook, when traveling especially, is my writing home. Where I check in, locate, take account. It's the interaction/intersection of the physical, hand, in time and in location and space. One locates oneself. And this act produces words which may or may not be "luminous" but are "there" in black on a white space. And it's an absolutely free space. Writing about past time, and present time, but always writing IN time, now time. I always begin with the date and the time. This is a record of entering into history, and however one writes, one *is* writing one's history. One day happens after another.

One needn't write much. Three or five lines a day can tell a lot. The famous journals of pioneer women crossing the West by wagon train marked by progress of miles, hunting for food, sickness, burial, birth, give a spare and eloquent history. No worry about literary style.

And it's that non-judgmental condition of writing that is so appealing. You are writing for yourself, and if *you* can't read your own writing back, it's time to find out what or how you want to write things. "Confessional" writing can be a very unburdening act, and is useful for clarifying confusing emotional situations. But if that is *all* you write down, it can become repetitious and tiresome.

Usually the more specific and detailed the writing is, the more grounded it feels later on, when memory has faded. Memory of the immediate present lasts only a few days before the selection process sets in, so get it while it's hot.

Try and be specifically responsive to your environment. Ask questions. Give the dignity of names to the generic plant, tree, bird, animal, etc. It takes the blur out. Find the nuances in your emotions so it's not love, hate, like, dislike, etc. Try writing in the third person to give some distance and space to a crowded "I."

Journal writing is often quick and notational, often like poetry. Gertrude Stein says, "A diary should be instantly like recording a telegram. A diary should simple be."

So it's your book and it's not plugged in to anything but you, and it's *portable*.

2000

New Millennium Trip to Pátzcuaro

January 6—February 7 2000

Remember next time the duffel
    bag is always too heavy

    Bring order to the new room at Casa Werma
    This house was given to Trungpa in the early
    70s & he wrote important texts here. A picture
    on the shrine of he and the Karmapa.
    I place a Sanskrit blessing there given me
    by a monk I found watching the sunset in Bolinas
    on New Year's Day who told me he was from
    Trungpa's Monastery in Tibet

Dream a Tibetan line dance—
  hop, step, cross-over

    Descending a perpendicular drop off a voice tells me
    pretend the wall slopes outward   Diamond steps appear
    'All time   contemporary in the mind'
    I find the previous owner buried under a large crystal
      in the center of the garden
        where many little werma spirits abound

In the Market~ 'I pay them whatever they want it's handmade'
  That's condescending. What if everything costs $1000.
    A good argument means a good time.
    Yearly average income in Mexico is $1500.

Visiting pyramids
      Place of the Coyote
        Place of the hummingbird
          built without draft animal or wheel

My adorable Cucaracha predates all the Gods

Back in Bolinas there is a hidden inlet
unspoiled and empty
I discover it frequently in dreams

In Guanajuato Guadalupe rings the door bell
This was a 16-dead-dog-by-the-roadside bus stop
For ten years the heads of the executed
revolutionaries hung on hooks at the corners
of the fort. Now eternal flames
burn in front of shrines for them
there, now a museum

Return to Pátzcuaro You can kill someone with witchcraft
if you also give them some arsenic

The present corporate stranglehold on the political system . . .
The U.S. American 'Drug Czar' General Barry McCaffrey is
quoted in today's Mexico City News as saying
"Mexicans are, by and large, better educated, better
dressed, and better behaved than Americans. But they
don't know where they're going. They're trying hard to
build structures." January 26, 2000

Sign in the supermarket

PANTY
DORIAN
GREY
LISA $8.33

Trungpa calls Mao Tse Tung a 'Cosmic Monster'
along with Hitler and Mussolini

LAW OF RIGHTS OF THE INDIGENOUS TOWNS & COMMUNITIES OF OAXACA "... to freely determine their existence and that codes in force recognize that manner of social and cultural identity ... the people have the Right to revitalize their customs and traditions ..."

Privatization of large pieces of agricultural land held by ejidos now sold to big companies. Lack of subsidies for campesinos competing with NAFTA usa prices for corn, etc.

January 30, 2000

It's so quiet
you can hear
the wasps sipping water
in the courtyard fountain

'Of course it's hard to imagine a couture client shelling out $25,000 so she can look like a bum'

One more bit of deconstruction like the Calvin Klein jeans treated to look dirty

—the new Galliano Spring-Summer 2000
haute couture show in Paris

At Viejo Gaucho

A couple in the corner across from us look like they are from a Casasola photo—he with a mustache, dignified ranchero appearance in dark suit, and absolutely wooden expression on his face, and drink with two straws untasted in front of him. She handsome faced with old fashioned dress, also with that expressionless demeanor of an earlier time, pulled back black hair.

The group on stage plays a Mercedes Sosa song, *Por Ti*; a Silvio Rodriguez piece *The Mask*,

Then 'Asta Siempre Che Guevarra'—the whole room sings along.   The Che legend, he's a deity,   'Please let me introduce you to Commandante Che Guevarra'.

"When I stopped painting and learned to write, I realized there is no longer a 'frame' around anything. I could go anywhere, from a speck of dust in the eye to a battlefield—JUST LIKE THAT!"

Evan Hunter (Ed McBain) (b. Salvadore Lombino)

Outside the door, the day's hairwashing, floor sweeping, bathing, coffee, sheep skins on the bamboo poles in the garden, airing out their smell.

A votive light for Douglas Oliver at the side nave of Jesus on the Cross. One man in solitary focus, prayer, at the front alter, his intensity overflows the room . . .

Mop mop mop every day the entire 100 yards down the corridor to the front door, THEN I can come back and mop your room.

"You are free to use abusive language to your mules, but that you should use such language to a colleague on an official matter does not flatter the institution with which you are connected."

Franz Blom to Sylvanus Morley

"Malinche was a hardboiled gold digger hungry for power"

—Franz Blom

Sign in Moralia airport says we are leaving—the United States—of Mexico

Plane is four hours late because of 'mechanical' problems. Flying over Oxnard look down to where flight from Vallarta crashed last week with all lost, really can't look down for long . . .

February 9 Bolinas

As morning gilds the skies
my heart awakening cries . . .

That familiar damp smell at dawn
Sparrows eat the plum blossoms

Old Dead Head
of sunflower still
stands propped
up in head high Kale
the Quail love to eat
so much

Interview with Tyler Doherty and Tom Morgan, from *For the Time Being: The Bootstrap Book of Poetic Journals*

Tyler Doherty and Tom Morgan: Your work—including recent collections like Again, *and the small chapbook* God Never Dies *as well as the poems collected in* As Ever*—shows a deep affinity to the journal form: attention to detail, a lively mix of overheard conversation, found language, dream & myth, political commentary, etc. Could you comment on what first attracted you to the journal form as a writer?*

Joanne Kyger: Writing happens in time and place and by the physical act of using the hand on paper or keyboard. So I feel it important to notate that actual time and place. I often compose directly on the keyboard (formerly known as the typewriter). I keep a fairly daily notebook, and often that is a resource for what turns out to be a piece of writing. Which I then date when I put it together.

By dating a piece of writing, I suppose that turns it into a "journal." Essentially one is writing down what is going on Now. What am I thinking Now. We are writing about past time or a future conjecture in a time Now. So I like everyone to know when that is. It grounds it for me. It says the writer is "present."

I never self-consciously thought of myself as using a "journal" form in writing. Certainly the broad scope of Williams' *Paterson* showed me that "poetry" can include all sorts of forms—letters, conversations, news articles—which was much more appealing than a book of "poems" which often lacked any narrative continuity.

God Never Dies was a daily practice of writing as a daily focus when I was in Oaxaca almost two years ago. It isn't a travel journal as such, more pieces of mood.

And of course, *Again* is arranged chronologically, like most of my published work, to show just that—chronology. That there is some kind of seasonal repetition, a progression of a life, lives, a story, a history, and the rather hollow attempt to attach a "meaning."

How about the importance of getting out and about and of taking the notebook with you?

The great thing about a notebook is that it is portable, easy to carry. An excellent place to make a home away from home when traveling. I often use a tiny notebook for on the spot walking observations. I like to use a blank page spiral-bound notebook so I can use it for drawings, paste ups, etc.—a kind of scrapbook.

Could you talk a little about where this push to dailiness comes from in your writing?

I think Charles Olson said "history is the memory of time." So the practice of writing down what's "going on" is a way of keeping history, memory of the immediate moment intact.

I live in a somewhat rural environment so the weather—clouds, winds, seasons, etc., are of utmost interest—the real movies. And of course it affects one's mental state. Try a month without sun and see how interior and depressed you can be. It's great today, the sun is out.

Otherwise I look out the glass door of my studio and watch the deer, quail, and other birds pass by. Easy to be a voyeur naturalist.

In the introduction to Strange Big Moon, *Anne Waldman links your writing to these Japanese poetic diaries, including Sei Shōnagon's* Pillow Book. *When you were writing your* Japan and India Journals *were you actively reading other Japanese poetic diaries and consciously incorporating their forms and styles or were there other, more significant, influences on this work?*

I didn't read Sei Shōnagon until the late '70s. There was not very much available in English translation of Japanese authors when I was living in Japan in the early '60s. Mostly my "journal" was a notebook in which I could keep a record of dreams, social occasions, trips, observations, etc. And then I tried out various ways of putting short "poetic" lines on the page. I never considered them "poems" and never published them. It was more like a working writing book. I was reading, through the American and British Cultural Libraries, books on Pound and Gertrude Stein, John Lomax, Carl Sandburg, etc. and had time to think over exactly what it was that the poetic voice/line was trying to achieve. Cid Corman, living in Kyoto then, was publishing his second *Origin* series, so work by Lorine Niedecker became known to me.

This "working writing book," as you call it, has over the years developed a sort of cult following and is now in its second edition. Why do you suppose so many people have been drawn to this admittedly unconscious collection of writings?

The *Japan and India Journals* are, I think, of interest because of the cast of characters involved. Ginsberg and his *Indian Journals* published from City Lights/Dave Haselwood Books, Snyder's trip published by Don Allen in the form of a letter to his sister, so people were interested in what I had to say about the trip. Trips to India were rarer in the early '60s, pre hippie trail. And as my Journals included my life in Japan too, it all got published together in one volume.

The recently published tribute to Philip Whalen, Continuous Flame, *contains excerpts from your correspondence with the late poet. Could you speak to his influence on you as a friend and writer? How instrumental was his example in the development of your aesthetic?*

Philip Whalen always dated his poems. I think it was a kind of formality of the moment. He did say once it was because he wanted others to know what he was thinking and doing at that time. Almost like "I got here first."

He was very encouraging to me as a writer, which was important to me as it would be to any young poet. Just keep on writing, he would say, when I asked for some kind of "critical" judgment. Which is what it's about anyway—writing as a "practice" and don't worry about whether it's "good" or "bad." There is a "voice" and hopefully an energy which gets off the page to the reader. Of course Philip's humor was very enticing, as was his agility of movement from voice to comment to voice on the page.

Could you trace back for us the history of the poetic journal as it's come down to you—both its Eastern and Western roots? Who were the first Western writers to specifically write in this form?

I'm not sure what you mean by the "poetic" journal. Bashō, certainly in his Haiku journey (1689) *Narrow Road to the Far North* (one of the various translations of the title). The *Tale of Genji* I read in 1962 while living in Kyoto, and although that reads like a piece of narration, it is a kind of journal/story of the times. Sei Shōnagon (born circa 965) of course with her lists, and incidents, is much more in the pillow book journal form.

Samuel Pepys starts his journal on January 1, 1660, which is a fabulous record of a very human person, but is not "poetic" in the usual sense of the word.

"Poetic Journal" is the term we've come up with to describe the cross section where poetry and journal writing meet. Is this appropriate or do you have another informal term you've used to describe this type of work?

The "style" of journal/notebook writing is really one of informality, intimacy. One is writing for oneself, whether or not there may be some future idea of publication. It can also have the intention of being an historical document, a chronicle of important events for the writer, in which case the writing is often more formal and self-conscious.

But journals usually carry a relaxed "tone." I consider it a completely free and open form, anything and everything can go onto the pages. The sense of being privy to the writer's more personal and intimate life is what can make the journal "exciting" reading. I recently finished reading Christopher Isherwood's journals, the result of a practice he kept most of his life, and they carry all the intimacy of his sexual life, his life in the spiritual practice of Vedanta, the politics of his relationship with English writers, American writers. He of course was a prose writer, a script writer, a journalist.

And he wasn't a poet. And I think you are more interested in Poet's Journals, in which the form is flexible, i.e., moving from prose lines into a more open form of words and space on a page, or whatever you want to call "poetry." Ginsberg's journals have all that variety.

It's really that mid-genre spot where the journals become poems and the poems become journals that's of particular interest to us. I think we started calling them "Poetic Journals" as a spin-off of the "poetic" in Earl Miner's Japanese Poetic Diaries. *(We were talking about that book a few years ago and started calling it "Japanese Poetic Journals" instead of "Diaries"). My assumption, gleaning what I can from our interview, is that you have always thought of your poems as poems and your journals as working notebooks to glean from as well as a place to write down unconscious accounts of daily life.*

I only considered the writing in the *Japan and India Journals* to be a kind of working writing book. Otherwise, I do consider the "poetic journal" a form in itself. I consider *Desecheo Notebook*, *Trip Out and Fall Back*, *Visit to Maya Land*, *Phenomenological*, *Wonderful Focus of You*, *The Dharma Committee* all examples of "poetic journals."

"Poetic journal" . . . for me it means a kind of movement back and forth from prose-like descriptive narrative bridges into shorter poem-like lines. Like the haibun style. And the element of time, happening in the moment, aware of the moment. Tight, spare. Etc. *Again* has chronological dates, but the narrative is submerged, no bridges.

Was there ever an aesthetic stance taken regarding writing / publishing this way?

As for the aesthetic stance in publishing such writing, I think it went along with the investigation into "open form" "projective verse", etc.—ways of putting voice and writing on the page that encouraged writers to publish these pages. Of course they were being written in notebooks all along, but at some point there was an awareness that these pages were OK as is, didn't have to be rewritten. And did this come out of a knowledge of the haibun page? The beats loved to practice haiku and read haiku, so it's likely.

Gary Thorp, a writer from this area, published a book in 2002 (Walker & Co) *Caught in Fading Light: Mountain Lions, Zen Masters, and Wild Nature*. He writes in a form of Japanese literature called Nikki Bungaku.

This is what he says about it: "literary diaries or journals are composed of separate, yet interrelated, short narratives that proceed in a continuous line from beginning to end, and which tell a sort of story. They contain nothing extra and are complete as they are. Historically the *nikki* form has always been quite liberating for writers. In its pages, a writer can behave as he or she wishes. The writing can consist wholly, or contain elements, of poetry, fiction, or nonfiction. . . . One is recording the mundane facts of an average day or journeying across a land never visited before. When poetry is produced, it is offered, not as embellishment, but as one of the natural facts of daily life."

2007

for Fall Equinox 03

DEER CROWN

for Joanne Kyger

NOT UNDERSTANDING. NOT CONSCIOUSNESS. JUST A DIAMOND,
OR A BRONZE LIGHTNING BOLT,
nestled in the center of a red rose
BALANCED
on the fine tip
of not knowing
while the emptiness of the jewel
roars out waves
of an aura
making mountains
with houses and trees.
-- A YOUNG BUCK
in his first mossy antlers
runs in the white fire
of the headlights
through the darkness
ahead of the car.

I'LL

BOW

TO
THAT
!

Michael

Love to Joanne & Donald

Interview with Chris McCreary, *Rain Taxi*

Chris McCreary: In your journals you wrote, "how very difficult to cut past and future time away from what is happening." What impact has it had on you to look back at these journals from 40 years ago, or to comb through your work to prepare your forthcoming Selected Poems*?*

Joanne Kyger: I think the past is something you need to practice remembering. Journals certainly revivify incidents from 40 years ago; when the new edition of the Japan and India journals came out last year, I read through the book like it was a story written by someone else. The further away from the past you are, the more resonance it has, becoming history. The act of dating what you are writing puts it in "time"—you realize you will be the future reader in a future time. Writing with the awareness of the "moment," dropping out of the loop of cause and effect. Although just recently someone read the book who was there in Japan and said, why didn't you tell me you felt that way about what I was doing! Allen Ginsberg, when he heard I was editing the journals said, don't take out the good stuff. I.e., be honest. So I did very little editing and of course no rewriting. The person of the writing is shown in all her emotional dimensions. It was a decision to make the intimate public, something which Allen was very generous with.

Similarly when I selected poems from 1964 to 2001, it was like reading a history of focus and story, the personas and adventures of my history. I really enjoyed it.

In a great letter that's included in the journals, you confess that you were at that time still "fundamentally middle-class at heart." How has that feeling changed over time—and how did it affect your writing?

"Middle-class" was a joke. I just wanted a lower profile while traveling with three "artistically" clad Americans in India, 1962. Actually Allen was adapting to the "India look"—long hair, beard, loose cotton shirts—a look that was to become familiar worldwide later on in the '60s.

When you hear of Nixon's election in 1960, you break into tears of frustration and write off America as a "lost cause." What scraps of hope has the country given you, if any, since then?

If I identified "with the country as a whole" I'd be a schizophrenic mess. I've always lived a West Coast, more or less rural, life. In this world, the emergence of a regional history has given us a language of geographical and environmental awareness. I can't make a psychic identity primarily as a USA citizen.

I think of myself as living on the North American continent, as living in a small coastal town that tried to become agriculturally self-sufficient in the '70s and continues to have a life of environmental awareness. The counterculture revolution of the late '60s and early '70s has continued with the maturing of aware relationships to "place."

The WTO demonstrations have revealed a challenging direction from a younger generation. I don't think that is going to stop. What people of this country express as their concerns and what government policy expresses are often at odds. I think the very form of our government with "a" president at the top is archaic, patriarchal, dangerous.

You cast some of the more monolithic figures of the Beat Generation in a sometimes less-than-flattering light, which I found refreshing; it helps humanize people whom younger poets have come to speak of as almost saintly, godlike figures over the years. Have you found it strange to watch Beat Culture take on such mythic cultural significance over time?

I of course was making private observations in my journals. These "Beat figures" were already in a "mythic" place when I met them. Kerouac's novels of the time—*On the Road*, *The Dharma Bums*—had already introduced them to enthusiastic readers and this gave them "national" identities which the media was quick to respond to. I think Ginsberg liked that because he had a lot to say publicly, about identity, politics, language. Kerouac wasn't really able to live in the public eye, be a spokesman.

Many of my favorite moments in the journals are descriptions of your dreams. Some are both amusing and a bit disturbing, like the one where Gary Snyder morphs into your mother. Yet while you recount the dreams in detail, you rarely attempt to interpret them. What do dreams mean to you, and how do they inform your waking, or your writing, life?

I believe dreams are just themselves, and say exactly what they say. You can interpret them on many levels and ways, and that is what is so wonderful about dream stuff. It's like poetry. You don't want to wreck it by saying this dream "means" this, when the dream is doing a beautiful job of reflecting what's going in your consciousness of the moment. Writing them down puts them in a readable and retrievable place; a year or years later the "meaning" is often more obvious. Strong dreams are often prescient, prophetic. The more you pay attention to your dreams, the more they tell you, and give you. I'm fascinated by their mobile energy, their inventiveness, of people you've never seen, rooms, places, incidents. I use dreams of the night before all the time to start off a piece of writing and often don't make any distinction between the dream and what is going on at the moment of writing in the "real" awake world.

One of my favorite Kerouac books is his *Book of Dreams*, first published in 1960 and still in print. They are so unabashed. The characters he writes about in his novels reappear in his dreams "and continue the same story which is the one story I always write about . . . and they reappear doing further strange things . . . And good because the fact that everybody in the world dreams every night ties all mankind together."

Dreams reflect the common urges of the heart, imagination, desire, domestic realities, fears, direct, like a telegram you dream it up. The dreamer dreams it up, but you don't own the language and images of dreams, they are common to everyone. So sometimes you dream someone else's dream—their broadcast frequency is stronger.

I thought Gary Snyder morphing into my mother was pretty weird too. Looking at it now, it's apparent I was leaving a marriage and going back to the matrilineal hearth for a while.

Each poem in your new book, Again, *bears a date, and many of the pieces really seem to capture a particular moment in time. Did you generally finish each poem on the same date it was started, or do these dates signify some other aspect of your poetics?*

Perhaps compulsively I always date all my writing, even to the hour sometimes. I feel writing is an occurrence, a happening, an intersection of the writer and time and place. The writing happens in the natural world of seasons, weather, tides. Where is the sun, where is the moon. This "real" world is there in concert with the writer's words, moods, muse.

The poem is written on the day it's dated, but often revisited later, when some light reshaping may happen.

I also find chronology, one day after another, a narrative, however subtle, of a story, of one's history.

Your poems have a sharp awareness of the people, places, and things around you, and the people who are mentioned in the poems often happen to be well-known poets. How does this naming of specific individuals inform the poems for you as the author? How would you like it to enrich the poems for the reader?

I live in a rather small coastal town north of San Francisco, and my writing reflects what goes on around me. Often neighbors are who I address thoughts, concerns, poems to, and they are sometimes writers, too.

Then again, writers, poets whose lives have been close to you are who often your dialogue is with. They may not necessarily be in your vicinity anymore, but they are where your thoughts go—your family as it were. From this comes an intimacy of tone which includes the reader. They are included in these anecdotal addresses.

My writing is usually about my life, the story I'm living. And there is a "cast of characters" that go in and out of my life, that I listen to, care about. It's that you aren't ever a solitary voice.

Your journals and poems address the ongoing desire to make your way in the poetry world and achieve recognition and respect from your peers. How do you think it's different now for a young poet to break into the literary scene? How big a role does gender play in the battle to be heard?

If you identify primarily by gender and let it get in the way of your "voice," it certainly can become a battle.

As a young writer, before my first book was published in 1965, I did want to be heard. But of course I had to write something first, find and develop my "voice." I've never had too much ambition in the larger world of recognition. And with those I consider my peers, there is mutual respect.

Young poets, like what happened to me, need to make their own literary "scene." It should be enjoyable, mutual, playful, supportive, and serious—responsive to the political times. But if it's not a pleasure, it's not poetry, to paraphrase William Carlos Williams. Poetry *is* a continuance of a lineage of poetry, and who "turns you on" becomes a teacher in a way no academy can teach.

The current accessible technology has produced many small presses, so there is lots of opportunity to see poems and books in print. I'd like to hear more of the physical poetry voice. The phrasing, the breathing, inflections, melodies—what words sound like in the actual air.

2000

School for Flowers

gold nasturtium –

five petals
with a dot
of orange
towards the center
and tiny refined
lines leading out
of those cunning blotches
on the two upper petals
back ended by a shooting star
tail

Treat this opening bud
with great consideration
It is close
to one who is on her journey
outward

Sunday July 19, 1998
for Nancy

When I step through the door
everything has changed, Finally
it is out the door
past homes, down the trail
the lovely beach,
draws me into her drawing. Finally
I am past the fear of life's paucity.
green Angels, stream, in hot California
And in the stillness seeds popping.

Joanne Kyger

Joanne Kyger Bibliography

The Tapestry and the Web (San Francisco, CA: Four Seasons Foundation, 1965)

The Fool in April: A Poem (San Francisco, CA: Coyote Books, 1966)

Joanne (Bolinas, CA: Angel Hair, 1970)

Places to Go (Los Angeles: Black Sparrow Press, 1970)

Desecheo Notebook (Berkeley, CA: Arif Press, 1971)

Trip Out and Fall Back (Berkeley, CA: Arif Press, 1974)

All This Every Day (Bolinas, CA: Big Sky, 1975)

Lettre de Paris [with Larry Fagin] (Berkeley, CA: Poltroon Press, 1977)

The Wonderful Focus of You (Calais, VT: Z Press, 1980)

Mexico Blondé (Bolinas, CA: Evergreen Press, 1981; with Donald Guravich)

Strange Big Moon: The Japan and India Journals. 1960–1964, (Bolinas CA: Tombouctou, 1981; reprinted North Atlantic Books, 2000; reprinted Nightboat Books, 2015)

Up My Coast (Point Reyes Station, CA: Floating Island Publications, 1981; illustrations by Inez Storer)

Going On: Selected Poems 1958–1980 (New York: Dutton, 1983)

The Dharma Committee (Bolinas, CA: Smithereens Press, 1986)

Man / Women: two poems [with Michael Rothenberg] (Pacifica, CA: Twowindows Press, 1987; illustrated by Nancy Davis)

Phenomenological (Canton, NY: Glover Publishing for Institute of Further Studies, 1989; illustrated by Donald Guravich)

Just Space: Poems, 1979–1989 (Santa Rosa: Black Sparrow Press, 1991; illustrated by Arthur Okamura)

Some Sketches from the Life of Helena Petrovna Blavatsky (Boulder, CO: Rodent Press & Erudite Fangs, 1996)

Pátzcuaro (Bolinas, CA: Blue Millennium Press, 1999)

Some Life (Sausalito, CA: The Post-Apollo Press, 2000)

Again: Poems 1989–2000 (Albuquerque, NM: La Alameda Press, 2001)

As Ever: Selected Poems (New York: Penguin, 2002)

Ten Shines (New York: Nijinsky Suicide Health Club, 2002)

The Distressed Look (Brunswick, ME: Coyote Books, 2004)

God Never Dies (Santa Cruz, CA: Blue Press, 2004)

Detektivgeschichten der Leidenschaft [with Stefan Hyner, epilogue by Jack Collom] (Berlin: Stadtlichter Presse, 2005)

Night Palace (Ellsworth, ME: Backwoods Broadsides, 2006)

About Now: Collected Poems (Orono, ME: National Poetry Foundation, 2007)

Not Veracruz (New York: Libellum, 2007)

Lo & Behold: Household and Threshold on California's North Coast (Voices from the American Land series; Placitas, NM: American Land Publishing Project, 2009; illustrated by Donald Guravich)

2012 (Santa Cruz, CA: Blue Press, 2013)

On Time: Poems 2005–2014 (San Francisco, CA: City Lights Books, 2015)

Amsterdam Souvenirs with Bill Berkson (Santa Cruz, CA: Blue Press, 2016)

Year of the Ram (San Francisco, CA: Omerta Publications, 2016)

Acknowledgments

Excerpted interviews were previously published in the following journals (reprinted with permission of the interviewers unless otherwise noted):

Watsky, Paul, "A Conversation with Joanne Kyger," *Jung Journal: Culture & Psyche*, vol. 7, no. 3 (August 2013). Reprinted with permission of the C. J. Jung Institute of San Fransisco. Carolan, Trevor, "Joanne Kyger: A Bloomsday Interview in NYC," *Pacific Rim Review of Books*, Issue 9 (Summer 2008). Russo, Linda, "Particularizing People's Lives: Joanne Kyger in Conversation with Linda Russo," *Jacket* #11 (April 2000, interview from February 27, 1999). Nahem, Lawrence, "A Conversation with Joanne Kyger." *Occident* 8 (Spring 1974); Anderson, Stephanie, "Stephanie Anderson with Joanne Kyger," *The Conversant* (October 2014); Middleton-McQuaid, Diana and John Thorpe, "Congratulatory Poetics: Joanne Kyger Interviewed," *Convivio* (1983); Smith, Dale (with Michael Price), "Energy on the Page: Joanne Kyger in Conversation with Dale Smith," *Jacket* #11 (April 2000; interview from May 4, 1997). Meltzer, David, "Joanne Kyger (1998)" appears in *San Francisco Beat: Talking with the Poets*, copyright 2001, reprinted with permission of The Permissions Company on behalf of City Lights Publishing. "Joanne Kyger in Conversation with Tyler Doherty and Tom Morgan" in *For the Time Being: The Bootstrap Book of Poetic Journals*, copyright 2007, reprinted with permission of Bootstrap Press. McCreary, Chris, "Interview: Joanne Kyger," *Rain Taxi*, vol. 6, no. 4 (Winter 2001). "Questions for Joanne Kyger from Anne Waldman" is reprinted by permission from *Civil Disobediences: Poetics and Politics in Action*, copyright 2004 by Coffee House Press.

"A Note on Joanne Kyger" and "Introduction to a Joanne Kyger reading in Buffalo, April 2, 1982" by Robert Creeley used with permission of Penelope Creeley on behalf of the Estate of Robert Creeley.

"It is lonely" "They are constructing a craft" "In July" and "from our soundest sleeps, it ends" first appeared in *The Tapestry and the Web* (Four Seasons Foundation, 1965) and later in *About Now: Collected Poems* (National Poetry Foundation, 2007). Excerpts from *The Japan and India Journals* (most recently published by Nightboat Books), copyright 2016 by Joanne Kyger. All reprinted with permission from the author.

Allen Ginsberg photo appears courtesy of the estate of Allen Ginsberg. Handwritten note by Ginsberg appears on the National Archives's copy: www.nga.gov/content/ngaweb/Collection/art-object-page.142149.html

Letter from Charles Olson (1968) appears courtesy of the Estate of Charles Olson and the University of Connecticut. Used by permission.

"Buzz Time" by Joanne Kyger first appreared in *Big Bridge* #9.

Letter from Paris (April 19, 1966), by Joanne Kyger & Larry Fagin, was originally published by Alistair Johnston, Poltroon Press, 1977.

Photos by Joanne Kyger (pages 39 and 41) are from *As Testimony: The Poem & the Scene* by Robert Duncan (White Rabbit Press, 1964).

The following letters and poems appear courtesy of the Joanne Kyger Archives at the University of California San Diego: "Letter from Lew Welch (Jan. 9th 1960)" reprinted with permission of the Estate of Lew Welch; "Letter from Philip Whalen" reprinted with permission of the Estate of Philip Whalen; "Frames" by Anne Waldman and "Deer Crown" by Michael McClure, printed with permission of the authors.

All other items are part of the author's private collection.

NOTE FROM THE EDITOR

I would like to thank those who took the time to interview Joanne, without whom this book would not have been possible. Thank you to Anne Valley Fox, who (years ago) gathered what turned out to be a pivotal selection of letters and poetry from Joanne's archive at UCSD. Thank you to Libby Hopfauf who assisted in gathering the interviews.

Thank you to Joshua Beckman, Heidi Broadhead, Patrick Dunagan, David Brazil, Duncan McNaughton, Matthew Zapruder, Garrett Caples, Rod Roland, Brian Marr, Donald Guravich, Hugh Cregg, Michael McClure, Anne Waldman, Alice Notley, David Meltzer, Ron Silliman, Norman Fischer, Peter Hale, Lynda Claassen, Melissa Watterworth Batt, Hoa Nguyen, Jared Stanley, Lisa Jarnot, Kevin Killian, Anselm Berrigan, Kevin Opstedal, Derek Fenner, Ryan Gallagher, Gordon Baldwin, Alastair Johnston, Alexander Moysaenko, Blyss Ervin, Kim Halstead, Nicole Hardy, Cameron Louie, and Jeff Clark.